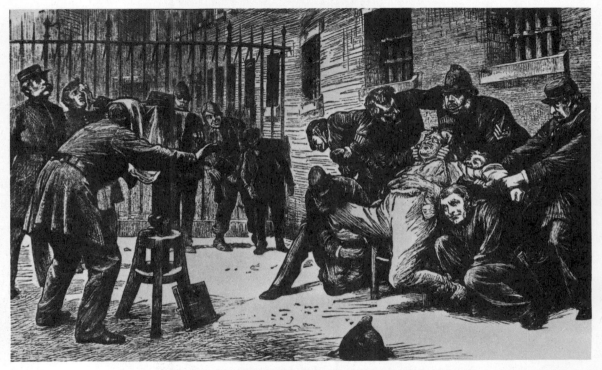

2   *A Newgate Scene, "Don't want his picture taken"*

THE AMERICAN PRISON:

from the beginning. . .

A Pictorial History

The American Correctional Association, *Publishers*

1 End papers, MARCHING IN LOCKSTEP

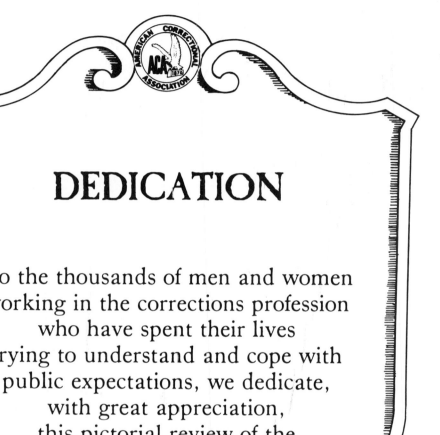

DEDICATION

To the thousands of men and women
working in the corrections profession
who have spent their lives
trying to understand and cope with
public expectations, we dedicate,
with great appreciation,
this pictorial review of the
American prison.

TABLE OF CONTENTS

Preface

Introduction

3 **Visiting in The Tombs, New York**

4 **Whipping post and pillory, New Castle, Delaware, 1868**

PREFACE

Nearly a decade ago, former ACA staff member William F. Bain conceived the idea of a pictorial history of the American prison. With the aid of David A. Kimberling, a prison inmate and photographer, Mr. Bain selected for reproduction many of the photographs included in this volume. These illustrations had accumulated in the archives of the Association over its history of more than a century.

Despite long hours of effort, the first manuscript produced by Mr. Bain failed to attract the interest of publishers. Meanwhile, the debate about the purpose and function of the correctional institution grew in intensity. The photos returned to the ACA archives. They undoubtedly would have remained in limbo were it not for the creative imagination of Anthony P. Travisono, executive director of the Association, who was convinced that the time for this book had indeed arrived. His enthusiasm was contagious and captured the energies of members of his dedicated staff.

All who contributed to the volume share the hope that this pictorial record will contribute to greater public understanding of the institution, which for most of its history, has been shrouded in mystery.

H.G. Moeller, President
American Correctional Association

Anthony P. Travisono
Executive Director/Editor-in-Chief

Diana N. Travisono
Managing Editor

Julie N. Tucker
Editor

Barbara Hadley Olsson
Editor

Ann J. Dargis
Associate Editor

William F. Bain
Originator of Editorial Concept

Chrystean Horsman
Research Assistant

Martin J. Pociask
Art Director

Alonzo L. Winfield III
Graphic Designer

Nancy M. LaFontaine
Graphic Designer

M. Eileen Burgess
Typographer

Graphics, typesetting and layout by ACA Services, Inc.

Printed by Optic Graphics Incorporated.

Excerpted with permission of Macmillan Publishing Co., Inc. from CORRECTIONS IN AMERICA:
AN INTRODUCTION, 2nd Edition, by Harry F. Allen and Clifford E. Simonsen.
Copyright © 1978 by Glencoe Publishing Co., Inc.

INTRODUCTION

Like any other institution in American history, the prison has changed substantially since its introduction in our society. Philosophies have varied, new ideas have come into vogue, fallen into disrepute, and re-emerged as the "answer" twenty years later. The prison has also evolved physically, reflecting America's history and advances in technology.

Despite the changes chronicled in this extensive collection of photos, certain conditions have been very constant. Resources have been in short supply from the very beginning; overcrowding has always been a problem; and an underlying public policy as a foundation to the institution's goals has been nonexistent.

We present this pictorial history to familiarize the public with the prison. Not all is being said; however, enough is here to reflect conditions of the past and hopes for the future.

It is not our intention to judge the practices graphically represented here. We are not the apologists of the past. Rather, we are among the architects of a much different correctional future as we try to lead public debate and policy decisions.

It is our hope that this pictorial history will stimulate greater public interest in corrections—and subsequently result in improvements in correctional institutions. Most important of all, it may hasten the development of sound institutions and acceptable community supervision programs.

Anthony P. Travisono
Executive Director
American Correctional Association

5 *Castle dungeon*

The European Influence on American Prisons

*It is insufficient to restrain the wicked by
punishment unless you render them virtuous
by corrective discipline.*

*Inscription over door of
Hospice of San Michele in
Rome, Italy, built in 1704.*

FROM A HISTORICAL PERSPECTIVE,

Imprisonment as a means of punishment is a relatively modern practice.

The earliest prisons, jails, and other places of confinement served primarily as centers for detaining common prisoners awaiting trial. The real punishment—death, mutilation, branding, or flogging—was meted out after the trial. Political prisoners' fates were determined while they waited in such places as the Tower of London, the Bastille in France, or Chillion Prison in Switzerland.

6 *Artist's conception of congreg confinement in early prison.*

Facts about early Roman places of confinement are sparse, the first known system was the vast Mamertine Prison (dungeons built under the main sewer of Rome in 64 B.C.). Most prisoners were confined in what were basically cages. Later, prisoners were kept in stone quarries and similar places originally created for other purposes.

Custom of Sanctuary

The Christian custom of sanctuary, or asylum, dates back to the 4th-century reign of Constantine. Wrongdoers were placed in seclusion, which was considered conducive to penitence. More formal places of punishment were developed during the Middle Ages within the walls of monasteries and abbeys as a substitute for imposing death sentences. Prisons built to lock up religious heretics during the Inquisition in the 14th and 15th centuries were similar in concept, if not in operation, to later cellular prisons in America. These early prisons, with

7   *La Garot*

their concept of reformation by isolation and prayer, had some influence on the first penitentiaries in the United States. With the development of gunpowder, fortress cities built in the Middle Ages were insufficient as defenses against roving bands of raiders. A new purpose was found for fortresses— housing political prisoners. Thus, the practice of long-term imprisonment was initiated, although prison chambers were not specifically included in castle plans until the 12th century.

Gaols

The construction of gaols (jails) was authorized in 1166 A.D. by the Assize of Clarendon (Constitutions of Clarendon). Called by Henry II, this step in the evolution of forms of imprisonment has a grim history.

Sheriffs often extorted huge fines by holding people in pretrial confinement until they gave in and paid. If the fine was not paid, they died in jail. No attempt was made to segregate prisoners by age, sex, or crime. Sheriffs typically sold food at exorbitant prices, forcing inmates without money to go hungry.

Bridewell Houses

An institution related to gaols was Bridewell, a workhouse built in 1557 for the employment and housing of London's riffraff. Bridewell was such a success that Parliament ordered each county to construct such an institution.

The proliferation of "Bridewell" houses in England was originally a humanitarian move intended to cope with the unsettling social conditions accompanying the breakup of feudalism and rapidly increasing urban populations. Comparable institutions soon appeared all over Europe.

8

Prisoners working at the tread-wheel; others exercising in the yard of the vagrants' prison, Coldbath Fields, England

Not merely extensions of almshouses or poorhouses, Bridewell houses were penal institutions for misdemeanants— ranging from pickpockets to prostitutes—who were compelled to work under strict discipline.

Oakum room, Middlesex House of Correction, Coldbath Fields, England

Workhouses

Although workhouses were intended to be used for the training and care of the poor, not as penal institutions, they soon became indistinguishable from Bridewells. Conditions and practices in both types of institutions steadily deteriorated, and by the turn of the 18th century these institutions were no more humane than the gaols.

PETITION TO THE GOVERNOR FROM NIBLO CLARK, A PRISONER IN DARTMOOR PRISON

Right Honourable Sir i humbly beg that you will listen to my woe
for what i Suffer in dartmoor prison the one half you do not Know
From repeated attacks of this frightful disease i am getting worse each day
So i humbly trust you will have me removed without the least delay

In making my request in poetry Sir i hope you wont think i am Joking
for the greatest favour you can bestowe upon me is to Send me back to Woking
For this damp and foggy Climate its impossible to ever get better
So i humbly trust in addition to this you will grant me a Special letter

Another little case i wish to State if you Sir will Kindly listen
has it would Cause a Vast amount of talk all round and about the prison
I mean if Niblo Clark Should be sent upon some public Works
it would cause more talk then the late dispute between the russians and the turks

in foggy wheather with my disease it would be impossible to larst one hour
and if you doubt the accuracy of what i say i refere to doctor Power
or any other naval doctor or one from plymouth garrison
they one and all would say the Same and likewise Doctor Harrison

Since my reception in dartmoor prison i have been a most unfortunate man
and i will tell you the why and wherefore as well as i possibly Can
for every time i been in this hospital its the whole truth what i Say
for my medical treatment i assure Sir i have dearly had to pay

A regularly marked man i have been for them all its well known to Captain Harris
for the list of reports against me would reach from dartmoor to paris
So i humbly beg Right Honourable Sir you will grant this humble petition
for i am sorry to State i have nothing to pay having lost both health and remission

Such Cruel injustice to poor Sick men is far from being just and right
but to report Sick patients in hospital is the officers Chief delight
But perhaps kind Sir you might imagine that they only do this to a dodger
But its done to all—George Bidwell as well and likewise to poor Sir Roger [Tichborne].

like Savage lions in this infirmary the Officers about are walking
to Catch and report a dying poor man for the frivolous Charge of talking
and when we go out from hospital our poor bodies they try to Slaughter
by taking those reports one at the time and Killing us on bread and water

I am suffering a Chest and throat disease a frightful Chronic disorder
and to go out from hospital is attempting Suicide to get heaps of bread and Water
for it is such cruel treatment made me as i am and brought me to the Verge of the grave

January 15, 1876

Excerpt from George Bidwell's *Forging His Chains*, 1888

10   **The Bastille, Paris, France**

Banishment was a popular punishment for serious offenders.

Each nation's royalty had its favorite place of exile for convicted prisoners: Russia's political exiles were sent to Siberia; Spain and Portugal's went to Africa. England's prisoners were sent to the American colonies and, following American independence, to Australia (approximately 134,000 between 1787 and 1875.)

France deported thousands of convicted prisoners to its penal colonies in French Guiana and New Caledonia. The horrors of French Guiana's infamous Devil's Island, once the world's most dreaded penal colony, did not end until it closed shortly after World War II.

11 *Dartmoor Convict Establishment, England, opened 1852*

Even though banishment removed thousands of prisoners to other continents, European prisons continued to be overcrowded and pestilent; the inmate death rate was staggering.

Men and boys in an early English prison

"School and a trade, or jail"

In the 17th and 18th centuries, overcrowding forced most European cities to convert some buildings into prisons. Mentally ill persons, women, children, criminals, and minor offenders—all were held in group cells.

Convict Hulks

Convict hulks were another method of dealing with overcrowding.
First used in the late 18th century as a temporary solution to prison overcrowding, the hulks, sometimes called "hell holds" or "floating hells," were broken-down war vessels and abandoned transport ships.

The hold of the ship

Stripped and anchored in bays and rivers throughout the British Isles, they were unsanitary, vermin-infested, unventilated, and run by keepers who flogged the inmates and forced degrading labor. The conditions were even worse than those in the gaols, houses of correction and workhouses of the time.

Prison ship "Success"

Disease ran rampant in the hulks, often wiping out entire prisoner populations and sometimes the crew and neighboring citizens as well.

This "temporary" solution lasted at least 80 years, with the last hulk maintained at Gibraltar as late as 1875.

In 1976, as prison populations began to increase significantly, three states—Washington, Maryland, and Louisiana—made extensive plans to use decommissioned U.S. Navy warships as prisons. The plans, however, were rejected. Again in 1980, some legislators in Massachusetts and New York made similar inquiries regarding the use of mothballed Navy ships. Again, the idea was rejected.

16 *Prison ship "Jersey" at anchor in New York harbor, 1776-1781*

17   *Whipping post and implements of torture aboard the prison ship "Success"*

18 *Convicts, in irons, praying near the "sweat box"*

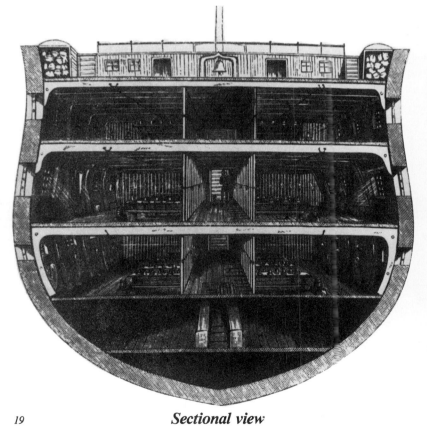

19   *Sectional view*
of the interior of the hulk "Defence"

13

The Gaol at Wymondham

Although many in American corrections have never heard of the Gaol at Wymondham in Norfolk, England, the Gaol changed the course of corrections in the United States.

Sir Thomas Beever
1726-1814

The Gaol at Wymondham was one of the relatively few gaols, or houses of corrections, that sought to comply with the reforms called for by John Howard in his State of Prisons published in 1777.

Erected in 1785, the Gaol embodied all the features Howard endorsed. Cells were provided to separate different types of offenders, and male and female inmates were kept in different parts of the building. Inmates not only slept but worked in separate cells. This solitary confinement was said by Sir Thomas Beever, creator of the Gaol, to be more effective than whipping and to be that part of punishment "from which reformation is chiefly expected."

This new arrangement was found to be wholly effective. With hard labor six days of the week, many prisoners earned more than double their maintenance, no punishment was necessary and the irons were never used.

The Gaol was also claimed to be a deterrent to crime, because circuit judges reported fewer commitments to the Gaol.

The work of Sir Thomas Beever in his new Gaol was described in a pamphlet published in 1790 by the Philadelphia Society for Alleviating the Miseries of Public Prisons. The Society proposed to reform the Walnut Street Jail in Philadelphia, as well as Pennsylvania's Penal Code. The pamphlet closed by declaring that what was needed at home was to follow this English example and "make our prisons Penitentiary Houses and places of correction." As a direct result of the pamphlet, the Pennsylvania Legislature passed the Act of April 5, 1790 which created the first penitentiary in the United States, if not the world, the Walnut Street Jail. With its philosophy of separate confinement at hard labor as the mode of discipline, it served as a model for the famous Pennsylvania System of prison discipline.

How the Philadelphia reformers heard of Sir Thomas' Gaol is still a mystery!

John Howard

The public neither knew nor cared about deteriorating prison conditions until the late 1700s, when Englishman John Howard began pushing for prison reform. Appalled by deplorable conditions in hulks and gaols when he found himself responsible for one, Howard pushed for legislative reforms to lessen the abuses and to improve sanitation.

Howard spent months visiting European prisons, documenting the conditions he found, and publicizing them through lectures and printed reports. *Modest* changes were initiated: the insane were removed from prisons, and women and children were either released or confined separately.

21 *John Howard*
1726-1790

In his European travels, John Howard was most impressed by Jean Jacques Vilain's Maison de Force (House of Enforcement) at Ghent, Belgium, and by the Hospice (asylum) of San Michele in Rome. An administrator and stern disciplinarian, Vilain was one of the first to develop a system of classification to separate women and children from hardened criminals, and serious from minor offenders. He opposed life imprisonment and cruel punishment, instead defining discipline by the biblical rule, "If any man will not work, neither let him eat." Vilain's far-reaching concepts of fair treatment, when viewed against the harsh backdrop of that era, mark him as a true visionary in the correctional field.

The individual cells and system of silence used by Vilain resembled procedures Howard observed at the Hospice of San Michele, built by Pope Clement XI in 1704. The hospice's philosophy was succinctly stated in the inscription over the entrance: "It is insufficient to restrain the wicked by punishment unless you render them virtuous by corrective discipline." Designed for incorrigible boys under 20, it was one of the first institutions to handle juvenile offenders exclusively, and still serves as a reformatory for delinquent boys.

15

Penitentiary Act of 1779

In 1777, Howard's reforms, as listed in his *State of Prisons,* led the English Parliament in 1779 to pass the penitentiary act, which provided for four major reforms—secure and sanitary structures, systematic inspection, abolition of fees for basic services, and a reformatory regime. The construction of the first penitentiary (at Wymondham in Norfolk, England) was a direct result of the act. Unfortunately, the act's lofty principles were hard to implement to a significant extent in the prevailing atmosphere of indifference.

The efforts of this energetic advocate for better prison conditions were cut short when he contracted jail fever (Typhus) and died in the Russian Ukraine in 1790.

John Howard's name is now synonymous with prison reform; he introduced the word "penitentiary" and the philosophy of penitence for one's crimes. The various John Howard societies commemorate his name and continue to press for reform in the United States and Canada.

As a result of Howard's influence, reformers in the United States vowed their jails would not follow Europe's tragic patterns. This was a commendable but unrealistic goal considering that American criminal law, based upon English common law, stipulated long sentences and imprisonment "at hard labor," patterns that still continue.

Visitor's side   *Prisoner's side*

22 **Friends visiting prisoners in an early English prison**

23 **Exercising at Pentonville Prison, England**

24 *Interior of an English convict prison*

25 *The Chapel in Pentonville Prison*

From Punishment to Correction

At the close of the 18th century, retributive punishment by the state was firmly entrenched in English and European laws. The work of philosophers in the 18th century's Age of Enlightenment made a devastating impact on the treatment of criminals. Great thinkers and movers such as Beccaria, Bentham, Montesquieu, Voltaire, Howard, and Penn contributed much to the recognition of humanity's basic dignity yet imperfection. Their humanitarian efforts led to the transition from punishment to correction, and formed the basis for modern penal philosophy.

26   *An American prison of 1776*

II Colonial America

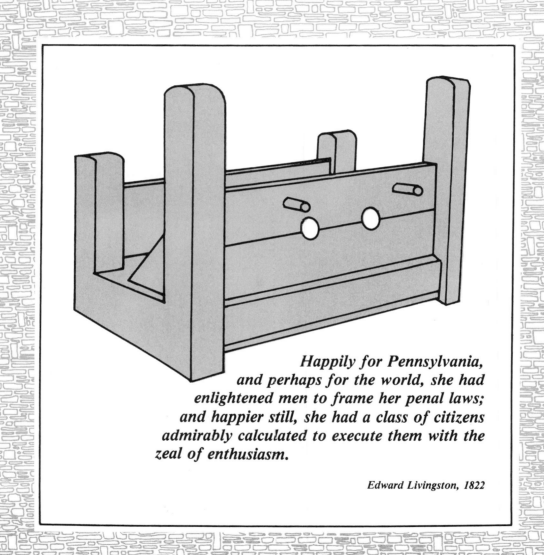

Happily for Pennsylvania, and perhaps for the world, she had enlightened men to frame her penal laws; and happier still, she had a class of citizens admirably calculated to execute them with the zeal of enthusiasm.

Edward Livingston, 1822

Hanging, burning at the stake, and breaking on the rack were among the ways of carrying out capital punishment for more serious offenses.

Soon after settlers arrived from England,

jails were used to detain those awaiting trial and for convicted persons awaiting the infliction of corporal or capital punishment. Often unsanitary and understaffed, they became a depository for men and women of all ages convicted for all types of crimes. The jails soon became overcrowded "hell holes" of disease, filth, vermin, and vice.

30   *Stone prison, Philadelphia, 1718*

The beginning of prison reform in the colonies can be traced to the arrival of William Penn in 1682 with a sizable land charter from Charles II. Penn established a penal code that retained the death penalty only in cases of homicide, and allowed the substitution of imprisonment at hard labor for former bloody punishments.

Penn's Code, aimed at deterring crime, had a number of significant provisions:

- All prisoners were to be eligible for bail;
- Those wrongfully imprisoned could recover double damages;
- Prisons were to provide free food and lodgings;
- The lands and goods of felons were to be liable for double restitution to injured parties; and
- All counties were to provide houses of detention to replace the pillory, stocks, and the like.

31 *Revolving pillory*

Chain gang at Richmond, Virginia

"Sanguinary Laws"

The principles underlying Penn's attempt to reform penal practice were not supported by Queen Anne, who succeeded Charles II. The laws were repealed by the Queen in council, only to be re-enacted by the Province of Pennsylvania, where they continued in force until Penn's death in 1718. The so-called "Sanguinary Laws," restored in 1718, remained in effect until the American Revolution.

A number of offenses were judged to be capital crimes, including treason, murder, burglary, rape, sodomy. buggery, malicious maiming, manslaughter by stabbing, witchcraft by conjuration, and arson.

One of the earliest efforts to operate a state prison for felons took place in an abandoned copper mine in Simsbury, Connecticut. This underground prison opened in 1773. It was established permanently as a state prison in 1790.

The first prison riots occurred there the next year as a result of "violence, poor management, escapes, assaults, orgies, and demoralization." Severe overcrowding also existed; 32 men slept in a room 21 feet long, 10 feet wide, and less than 7 feet high. The prisoners were secured with iron fetters around the ankles. While prisoners were at work, a chain fastened to a block was locked to these fetters or around prisoners' ankles. The punishments meted out were relatively harsh compared to modern sentencing practices; "burglary, robbery, and counterfeiting were punished for the first offense with imprisonment not exceeding ten years; second offence for life."

26

33 Newgate Prison, Connecticut

This "mine shaft" prison has sometimes been referred to as the first state prison, yet, in reality, it was more akin to the sulphur pits of ancient Rome.

34   ***Copper coins mined at Simsbury***

"If the sweet Muse, with nature's best control,
Can melt to sympathy the reasoning soul,
Shee bids thee rend those *grating bars* away,
And o'er the dungeons break the beam of day:
Give the frail felon with laborious toil
To pay the penance of his wasted spoil.
Hear his deep groan, heed his repentant prayer,
And snatch his frenzied spirit from despair;
Nor let those fields, arrayed in heavenly bloom,
Blush o'er the horrors of a *living tomb!**

*Extract from a poem written by a lady of Boston, in 1797, after visiting Newgate Prison. It indicated the great notoriety and formidable character which Newgate had obtained, in the opinion of the benevolent and gifted poetess."

35   ***Ruins of Newgate Prison***

The Walnut Street Jail

36   *The Walnut Street Jail, Philadelphia 1790*

The first true correctional institution in America was started in Philadelphia in 1790 and known as the Walnut Street Jail. The same year, Philadelphia Quakers renewed their efforts to change the treatment of convicted criminals. They persuaded the Pennsylvania legislature to declare a wing of the Walnut Street Jail a penitentiary house for all convicted felons except those sentenced to death.

37   *First sermon preached in the jail by Rev. William Rogers, 1787*

38 *Prune Street Debtors' Jail, 1838*
Imprisonment for debt was legally abolished by
the Act of July 12, 1842 in Pennsylvania.

40 *Stamp issued to help finance*
the building of the Walnut Street Jail

39 *Jean Pierre Blanchard takes off from the jail yard*
in the first balloon ascension in America.

Unlike the workhouses, prisons, and jails already in existence, the Walnut Street Jail was used exclusively for the correction of convicted felons. The system of discipline, developed through the ideas and efforts of such reformers as Dr. Benjamin Rush, became known as the "Pennsylvania System."

Dr. Benjamin Rush

Dr. Benjamin Rush
1745-1813

Dr. Rush, who lived from 1745 to 1813, was a prominent physician, political leader, member of both Continental Congresses, and a signer of the Declaration of Independence. He believed that prisoners should be housed in a large prison building equipped with individual cells for dangerous and assaultive prisoners and apartments for the remainder of the inmate population.

Dr. Rush also believed prison systems should include gardens so prisoners could obtain both food and exercise. He also insisted that prison industries should provide salable products to the outside market in sufficient quantities to support the prison system. He thought the purpose of punishment of prisoners was as follows:

- To reform the person who suffers punishment;

- to prevent perpetration of crimes; and

- to remove those persons from society who have manifested, by their tempers and crimes, that they are unfit to live in society.

Independence Hall, Philadelphia

The Pennsylvania System

Many of Dr. Rush's ideas were incorporated into the Walnut Street Jail's "Pennsylvania" system of discipline. The system called for solitary confinement without work. It was assumed that offenders would be more quickly repentant and reformed if they could reflect on their crimes all day. As the negative physical and psychological effects of this isolation soon became apparent, work (usually piecework or handicrafts) was introduced, along with moral and religious instruction.

Despite the promise of its beginning, poor planning led to the breakdown and ultimate failure of the Pennsylvania System. Nevertheless, the Walnut Street Jail had a permanent and pervasive influence on the development of correctional institutions around the world.

43 *Jeremy Bentham*
1748-1832

The "Panopticon" Plan

Dr. Rush and other reformers
combined the ideas of both John
Howard and Jeremy Bentham, English
architect, philosopher, and idealist. In
1799, the British Parliament contracted
with Bentham to furnish the design for
an innovative prison.

Bentham's "Panopticon" plan called for
a huge structure covered by a glass roof.
A central cupola allowed the guards to
see into the cells, which were arranged
like spokes on a wheel. Bentham
believed that the visibility would make it
easier to manage the inmates.

Although the British government did not
follow Bentham's plan in its
construction, several U.S. prisons used
his ideas. The last institution based upon
his "Panopticon" plan was Stateville,
Illinois in 1919.

44 *Prison at Richmond, Virginia, erected 1800; Bentham's "Panopticon" plan used.*

45 *Newgate Prison, New York*

Newgate Prison, New York

In 1797, Newgate Prison was opened in New York City, adopting many of the ideals of the Pennsylvania System. Prison industries paid nearly all the prison's expenses during its first five years. Its warden, Thomas Eddy, established job descriptions for staff assignments and set out to hire those who could qualify for defined positions.

Eddy required a planned, adequate diet with daily menu changes. He established the first prison hospital and pharmacy and hired the first full-time physician and pharmacist. He and his family initiated the policy to live within the prison as an example to inmates and staff members.

Eddy conducted an evaluation of those sentenced to Newgate and after several years stated that no more than one in 10 of those confined there required the security provided by the walled institution. Eddy believed that if crime was to be reduced, its inciting causes must be reduced.

First Prison Reform Society

American prison reformers, partly motivated by John Howard's work in Europe, began investigating American jails and quickly discovered conditions parallel to those Howard discussed in his works.

The first prison reform society in America or Europe was the Philadelphia Society for the Alleviation of the Miseries of Public Prisons founded in 1787. The Society's purpose was to alleviate the miserable physical and social conditions of the public jails. The principal duties of the Society, which exists today as the Pennsylvania Prison Society, were to visit the public prisons once each week; to inquire into inmates' circumstances; to report abuses; and to examine the influences of confinement or punishment on society's morals.

Bright Hope

As the 18th century drew to a close, the move for prison reform was sparked by new vigor and energy. The decade after the Walnut Street Jail opened was full of bright hope for the concepts embodied there, however imperfectly. Besides the Walnut Street Jail, there were many other attempts to establish prisons for convicted felons.

State Prison at Charlestown, Massachusetts in 1805

46

"The Big Houses"

With the industrial age came overcrowded prisons, which forced administrators to consider much larger and more productive institutions. As America entered the 19th century, it also entered an age of bigness and expansion. The prison movement adopted this growth-oriented philosophy and the 19th and early 20th centuries became the age of "The Big Houses."

Maryland State Penitentiary, built in 1811

47

48 *"The Closed Door,"
1800s prison cell in the
Old Penitentiary, New York*

49   Convicts retiring to their cells, 1852

The Auburn and
The Pennsylvania Systems

III

*Our Penitentiaries
are so many schools
of vice; they are so many
seminaries to impact lessons and maxims
calculated to banish legal restraints,
moral considerations, pride of
character, and self regard.*

*from REPORTS OF THE PRISON
DISCIPLINE SOCIETY, Boston 1826-1835
George W. Samson*

Two parallel correctional philosophies affecting the nature of American prisons emerged in the early 19th century. These systems, the Auburn and the Pennsylvania, were based on the belief that regimens of silence and penitence would prevent cross-infection and encourage behavior improvement in prisoners.

51   ***Eastern State Penitentiary, 1829....***

50   ***John Haviland***
1792-1852

The **Western State Penitentiary** at Pittsburgh was built in 1826, based on the cellular isolation wing of the Walnut Street Jail in Philadelphia. This proposed octagonal monstrosity provided for solitary confinement and no labor. The legislature amended the program in 1829, maintaining solitary confinement but adding the provision that inmates perform some labor in their cells. In 1833, the small, dark cells were torn down and larger outside cells were built. These efforts influenced the development of the Eastern State Penitentiary in Philadelphia.

The Pennsylvania System

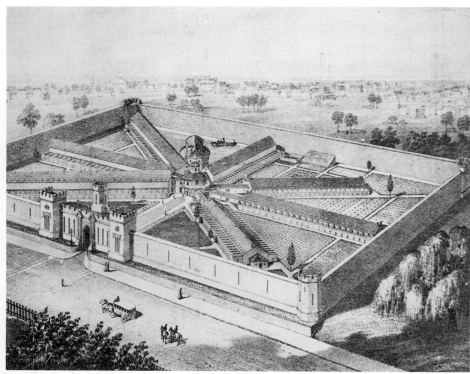

52   *...a bit later...*   53   *...in 1958, surrounded by the community*

The Eastern State Penitentiary, designed by John Haviland and completed in 1829, became the model and primary exponent of the Pennsylvania "separate" system. The prison had seven original cell blocks radiating from the hub-like center, a rotunda with an observatory tower, and an alarm bell.

A corridor ran down the center of each block with the cells at right angles to the corridor. Each cell had a back door to a small, uncovered exercise yard and double front doors, the outer one made of wood, and the other of grated iron with a trap so that meals could be passed to prisoners.

54 *Michael Cassidy*
Warden from 1881-1900

Eastern State Penitentiary

55 *The Iron Gag*

56 *Eighth and ninth blocks at*
Eastern State Penitentiary, 1884
One hundred rooms, 18 x 8 feet,
16 feet high

Roberts and Richard Vaux

In the list of famous fathers and sons engaged in penal reform, Roberts and Richard Vaux should be given special attention. These two famous Philadelphians' influence on penology and prison administration lasted for nearly a century.

58   *Roberts Vaux*
1786-1836

57   *Richard Vaux*
1816-1895

Roberts Vaux devoted his life to humanity as a memorial to his sister. Vaux joined the Philadelphia Prison Society and was a member of many of its committees. As one of the Society's corresponding secretaries, he carried on a lively correspondence with European and American penal reformers. Vaux contributed the vast knowledge of corrections he acquired to the radical penal experiment of his day—the Pennsylvania system. He advocated solitary confinement day and night with books and labor as the means for reforming prisoners.

Vaux became well-known in Europe as a penologist, philanthropist and educator. When he died, his colorful son Richard continued his work but in a much more militant manner than his father. As chairman of the Board of Inspectors of the Eastern State Penitentiary at Philadelphia for 40 years, Richard Vaux was an uncompromising advocate for the separate system of prison discipline.

The introduction of handicrafts in the solitary cells in **Pennsylvania** and the factory system in the congregate workshops of other states were extensions of the industrial program of early American prisons. They embodied no new principle of trade training as treatment for crime. Under pressure to make the prison self-supporting, wardens in this era had to be concerned as much about profits as prisoners.

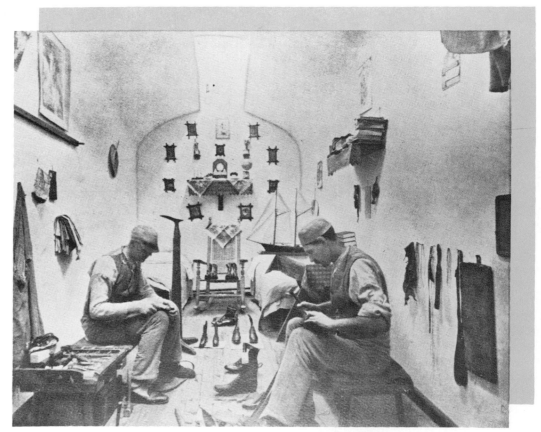

59

A room in ninth block, making shoes

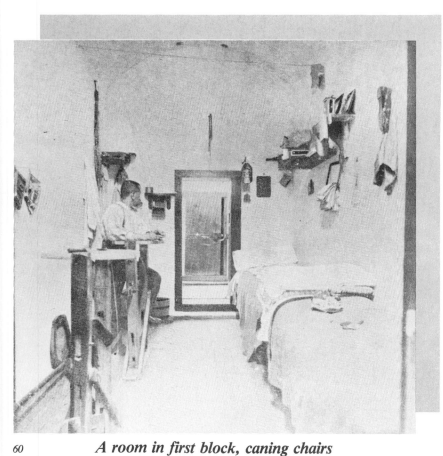

60   *A room in first block, caning chairs*

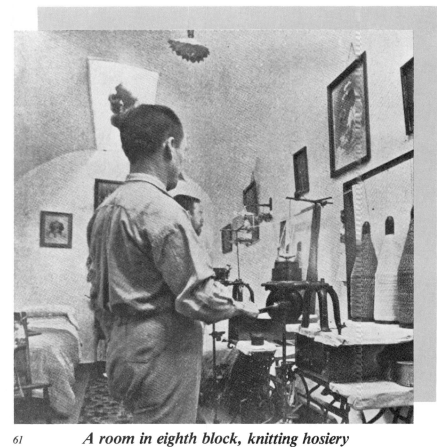

61   *A room in eighth block, knitting hosiery*

There was no real force behind either moral or academic instruction

for the vast majority of prisoners, although during this period chaplains were appointed at most prisons. Sabbath schools were organized to teach bible lessons as well as reading and writing. The wide distribution of bibles and the holding of revival services in various prisons represent the principal efforts of this period to apply a definite therapy (other than punishment) to the criminal tendencies and habits of offenders.

A Whole New Discipline

In the development of 30 or more prisons during this period, the added element of silence was used to maintain the penitentiary system and aid the reformation of the criminal. Along with silence came a whole new prison discipline.

62   *Convicts at worship in an English prison*

63   *Convicts at dinner in an English prison*

Prisoners returning from work on Blackwell's Island, New York, 1876

In line waiting to be flogged

They ate in silence "face to back" to prevent communication through signals; they stood with folded arms and downcast eyes when an officer approached; they did not gaze at or communicate with visitors (they were allowed only a limited number of visitors under strict supervision); their communications through letters with the outside world were strictly limited; and they were allowed few, if any, newspapers. They lived "in a prison within a prison," in interior cells, which made contact with the outer world difficult.

This discipline meant that prisoners did not communicate with each other; they walked to and from work or meals in lockstep so as to show both hands to the guards at all times.

The cells were intended to contain only one prisoner. Soon after the penitentiary was opened, however, separate confinement without exposure to or communication with other inmates became an obvious impracticality. The prisoners developed ingenious methods of communication, such as tapping codes on water pipes. Doubling up prisoners became necessary because the prison's population quickly surpassed legislative appropriations for construction.

The Pennsylvania System in Canada

An example of the Pennsylvania system in Canada is described by the late Alex Edmison, a noted Canadian humanist, educator, and penal reformer. Edmison recalled that Charles Dickens referred to Kingston Penitentiary in 1842 as "...an admirable jail, well and wisely governed and excellently regulated in every respect." The institution's rules and regulations were strenuous for staff and inmates alike. The warden had to attend to the prison constantly. The guards were to be on duty from 5:00 in the morning until 6:30 in the evening, seven days a week, from the beginning of April to the end of September. "During the remainder of the year, the hours for continuing the prison open, shall embrace all daylight." The guards had to "preserve unbroken silence" between the inmates, who "must not exchange a word with one another under any pretence whatever and must not exchange looks, wink, laugh, nod or gesticulate to each other." The convicts were to yield "perfect obedience and submission to their keepers" and were, at all times to "labour diligently."

Corporal punishment was inflicted for the willful violation of any of these duties. It is reported that a 10-year-old inmate, Peter Charbonneau, who was committed in 1845, was lashed repeatedly for such violations. "Charbonneau's offences were of the most trifling description such as were to be expected of a child of 10 or 11, like staring, winking, and laughing, and for these, he was stripped to the shirt and publicly lashed 57 times in 8½ months."

Kingston Penitentiary, opened 1835

66

The Auburn System

In 1816, New York began the construction of a new prison at Auburn. It was patterned after other early American prisons with a few solitary cells to conform to the law of solitary confinement to be used for punishment, and with sizeable night rooms to accommodate most prisoners.

Auburn Prison, New York 1868

To test the efficiency of the Pennsylvania System, an experiment was tried in 1821 with a group of inmates who were confined to their cells without labor. Many of these inmates became insane and sick. The experiment was abandoned as a failure in 1823, and most of the inmates studied were pardoned.

A new plan was adopted whereby all inmates were locked in separate cells at night, but worked and ate together in congregate settings in silence under penalty of punishment.

The builder of this prison, for reasons of economy, built the cells back to back in tiers within a hollow building, the doors of the cells opening out on galleries that were 8 to 10 feet from the outer wall. Thus developed the interior cell block, which has become one of the unique characteristics of American prisons.

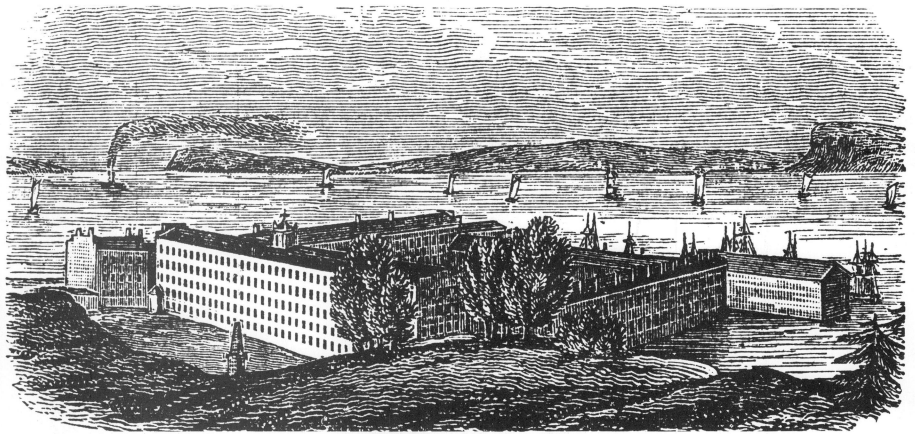

Sing Sing Prison, New York, 1840

This plan of cellular confinement at night, usually in interior cell blocks, with silent labor in congregate workshops by day, became known as the Auburn system.
The Auburn system became the pattern for over 30 state prisons in the next half-century, including Sing Sing Prison at Ossining, New York in 1825.

Connecticut built a model prison based on the Auburn system at Wethersfield in 1827.

70 Troy, New York

Prison reformers of this period were repelled by the punishments at Auburn and Sing Sing, and the prison at Wethersfield became the model of the Auburn system in America. In 1829, Massachusetts opened a cell block for the separate confinement of 304 prisoners, and Maryland built a wing with 320 exterior cells, formally adopting the Auburn system. Vermont, New Hampshire, and Ohio followed with new cell blocks patterned after Auburn. In the 1840s, Georgia and Kentucky also converted to the Auburn system. Thus, all the early American prisons, except those in Pennsylvania, adopted the Auburn System. Subsequently, from 1825 to 1870, 23 new state prisons were built after the Auburn plan in the United States.

50

71 Joliet Penitentiary, Illinois

72 Water and slop buckets clean and ready for inspection

Silence and Penitence

The guiding ideology in both the Pennsylvania and Auburn systems was the belief that a regimen of silence and penitence would prevent cross-infection and encourage behavior improvement in prisoners.

Supporters of the Pennsylvania system claimed it was superior because the system made it easier to control prisoners, gave more consideration to their individual needs, prevented "contamination" by complete separation of prisoners from each other, and provided more opportunity for meditation and repentance. It was also claimed that prisoners could leave the system with their background known only to a few administrators.

On the other hand, supporters of the Auburn, or congregate, system argued that it was cheaper to construct and implement, provided better vocational training, and produced more money for the state. The persuasiveness of economics finally decided the battle, and the congregate system was eventually adopted in almost all American prisons, even in Pennsylvania.

73 *New south wing cell block, Auburn, New York, 1934*

51

74 *An unidentified cell block showing an early all steel walkway system.*
Bare wires "roughed in" on the ceiling of
the lower walk for electricity to be installed.

Architecture, programs, and often punishments were substantially **institutions.** Each had multitiered interiors; dimly lit cells; a program of daily work, Sunday religious service, and Sabbath school; prisoner uniforms; a meager and monotonous diet; ever-changing politically appointed personnel; petty rules, and severe punishments.

rules, regulations and the same in all these

75 *Jefferson Prison, Indiana. Erected in 1847, replacing a wooden stockade built in 1822 which had been Indiana's first prison.*

Prison Stripes

The use of prison uniforms was also initiated at Auburn and Sing Sing. Different colors were used for first-time offenders and for repeaters. These outfits served to reveal the prisoners' classification at a glance, and to facilitate identification of escapees.

The famous "prison stripes" appeared in 1815 and only recently (1950s) were discarded in most prisons. By preventing relationships among prisoners, which were viewed as the source of chaos in early American prisons, each system sought by different means to maintain the penitentiary system, and avoid a general return to capital and corporal punishment.

76 *In line at Auburn, New York, 1840*

A Silent Public

Silence characterized not only prisoners but the public, which became less and less disturbed by prison problems and activities. The "out of sight, out of mind" public attitude was especially evident in 19th-century prisons. Most were located in the countryside, free from either interference or inspection by the communities supplying prisoners.

It is not difficult to understand why rules and procedures emphasized the smooth and undisturbed operation of the prison rather than efforts to modify the individual prisoner's behavior. Administrators were judged by the prison's production record and the number of escapes, not by the number of inmates rehabilitated. Because of this prevailing spirit, rules were designed to keep prisoners under total control.

If there were disturbances in the prisons, it was difficult to penetrate the walls of the new interior cell blocks; and under the system of solitary cells, trouble was soon confined to the individuals involved, who were properly handled by officials. The legislatures were especially satisfied when the new factory system of production began to show a profit. The penitentiary system was assured its place in public administration.

The industrial phase of prison administration became so important that discipline was exercised to ensure optimal production levels. The arguments between the advocates of the Pennsylvania and Auburn systems subsided for lack of fuel. The Auburn system prevailed over the Pennsylvania system because it provided superior industrial returns. The silent system continued in many prisons beyond this period and vestiges of it still persist. But its original purpose, the prevention of cross-contamination of inmates, was forgotten. It was maintained in some prisons simply because it was easier to run an institution where the inmates were seen but not heard.

The Report contains the following comparisons in regard to the productive labors of the inmates of the prisons of several different States:

I. *In regard to the PRODUCTIVE INDUSTRY of each convict:*

In Auburn prison, each convict earned in 1849	$106.93
In Sing-Sing, male prison, each convict earned in 1849	100.69
In Sing-Sing, female prison, each convict earned in 1849	29.65
In Maine State prison, each convict earned in 1848	83.00
In New Hampshire prison, each convict earned in 1848	30.91
In Vermont Prison, each convict earned in 1848	70.72
In Massachusetts prison, each convict earned in 1848	107.38
In Rhode Island prison, each convict earned in 1848	49.00
In Connecticut prison, each convict earned in 1848	90.00
In New Jersey prison, each convict earned in 1848	92.19
In new Penitentiary, Phila., Pa., each convict earned in 1848	43.00
In Ohio State prison, each convict earned in 1848	93.54

II. *In regard to expenses for ordinary support, excluding salaries of officers:*

In Auburn prison, average of each convict, 1849	51.75
In Sing-Sing male prison, average of each convict, 1849	48.49
In Sing-Sing female prison, average of each convict, 1849	91.38
In Maine State prison, average of each convict, 1848	70.82
In N. Hampshire prison, average of each convict, 1848	65.16
In Vermont prison, average of each convict, 1848	60.87
In Massachusetts prison, average of each convict, 1848	51.00
In Connecticut prison, average of each convict, 1848	63.00
In New Jersey prison, average of each convict, 1848	63.00
In new Penitentiary, Phila., Pa., average of each convict 1848	43.00
In Ohio State prison, average of each convict, 1848	43.00

III. *In regard to the earnings of each convict over his expense, not including salaries:*

In Auburn prison, 1849	45.30
In Sing-Sing male prison	51.11
In Maine State prison, 1848	12.18
In Vermont prison, 1848	8.30
In Massachusetts State prison, 1848	46.71
In Connecticut State prison, 1848	39.00
In New Jersey State prison, 1848	28.78
In Ohio State prison, 1848	30.90

IV. *In regard to prisons where the earnings of each convict fall short of his expenses, exclusive of salaries:*

In Sing-Sing female prison, 1849	$62.75
In New Hampshire State prison, 1848	11.34
In new Penitentiary, Phila., Pa.	17.00

Excerpt from Annual Prison Report for New York, 1850

Model for 150 Years

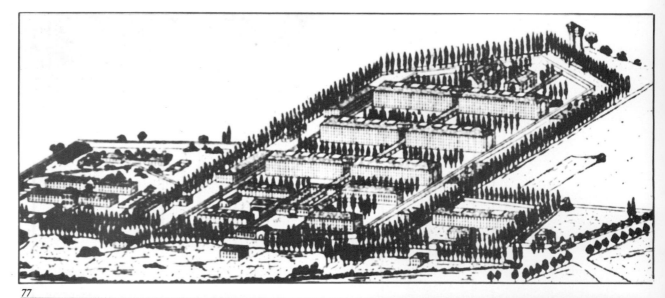

77

Auburn's structural design—inside cells and wings composed of cell tiers (cell blocks)—became the model for most prisons built in the following 150 years. Variations of the Auburn concept are numerous, the most popular being the "telephone pole" design. Regardless of the cell block arrangement, the inside-cell design became the most prevalent model in America.

Prison at Fresnes, France, 1898. The parent institution of the telephone pole design (top)

Erie County Penitentiary, New York, (bottom)

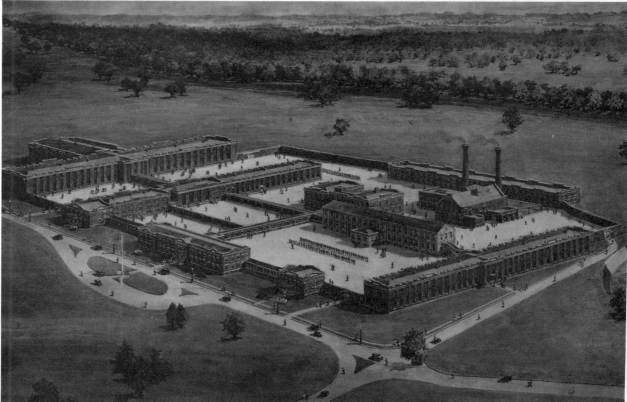

78

CLINTON STATE PRISON, 1868.

STATISTICS, 1868.—Location, at Dannemora, 16 miles north-westerly from Plattsburgh, 1700 feet above level of Lake Champlain.   Established 1844.   Area of prison enclosure, 37 acres. Wood-lands for supply of charcoal, (mostly over mountains) about 17,500 acres.   Valuations,—Real, $465,467.66; Personal, $460,349.65; Total, 925,817.31.   Average number of Convicts for the year, 518.   Occupation,—Manufacturing Iron and Nails for the State, 352; Tailors, Shoemakers, Carpenters, Laborers, Cooks, &c., 149; in Hospital, and : disabled, 11 : Total, Sept. 30, 1868, 512·

REFERENCES.—A, Prison Dormitory, 500 feet long, 50 feet wide, (in the clear) containing 544 Cells.   B, Kitchen, Dining Hall and Storeroom in 1st Story, Chapel, Guard House and Armory in 2d story, Hospital in 3d story.   C, Offices of Agent and Warden, Clerk and Manufacturing Department.   D, Agent and Warden's Dwelling.   E, Forge Shop.   F, Engine Room and Coal House. G, Dwelling for Clerk and Principal Keeper.   H H, Coal Kilns.   I, Rolling Mill.   J, Nail Factory.   K, Guard Post.   L L, Machine and Carpenter Shops.   M, Ore Separator.   N, Chaplain's Office and Library and Tailor Shop.   O, Store.   P, Old Shoe Shop (used as a Store House).   Q, Hall Mine.   R, Thomas and Watson Mine.   S S, Tram Railroad.   T T, Plank Road over mountain to Coal Kilns and woodlands, and to Ellenburgh (built by the State).   Production in 1868: 45,146 Kegs of Nails and 80 Tons of assorted Merchant Iron.   Consumed about 900,000 bushels of Charcoal.

A Fifty-Year Struggle

The 50 years that followed the opening of Auburn Prison were years of great activity in prison development and administration, but years that did not produce many lasting contributions to penology. The rule of silence, the chief experiment of this period, was abandoned in favor of more normal living conditions. The system of prison discipline that accompanied noncommunication degenerated into nothing more than a cruel and inhuman system for enforcing prison officials' singular ideas of what discipline was to be.

The greatest contributions, which persisted for nearly 100 years, were prison industries programs and interior cell blocks. However, even these have proved to be liabilities. The contract and lease system that formed the basis of the industrial program in this period required a tremendous 50-year struggle before the evils they produced were eliminated. As a means of safekeeping a comparatively few dangerous or disturbed inmates who required unusual means of confinement, the interior cell block may have been justified; as for the indiscriminate housing of thousands of prisoners who did not need escape-proof steel cages, it had no economic or penal justification.

80   *Marching in lockstep, Joliet Penitentiary, Illinois, 1900*

One of the more important, but less noted, aspects of the early prison architecture was the grand scale and sheer size of these institutions. "Bigger is better" (and cheaper) was the slogan of early prison builders. These huge, gothic-style structures achieved an effect similar to the cathedrals of Europe in the Middle Ages—that of making the people inside seem small and insignificant. This feeling was further enhanced by the systems of severe discipline employed in these huge castles. Also, the size of these early prisons gave rise to subtle pressure to keep them filled with society's castoffs.

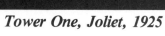

Tower One, Joliet, 1925

The Civil War

No history of corrections would be complete without mentioning prisons used during the Civil War.

Both sides were baffled as to how captured prisoners should be treated. Neither did very well and consequently thousands upon thousands of Union and Confederate soldiers died between 1861 and 1865.

Andersonville and Ft. Delaware, two of the better known facilities, were used extensively when America was at war with itself.

Several books have been written about this sordid episode in American history. We present a brief view of that history.

82   *Andersonville Prison, Georgia, 1865*

General John Hunt Morgan

It was a classic escape, one that even Hollywood wouldn't need to embellish. In a newspaper account that thrilled the South and shocked the North during the Civil War, the headline read

"MORGAN, 6 OTHERS, FLEE PRISON"

Columbus Ohio. Nov. 28, 1863—Confederate Gen. John Hunt Morgan and six of his captains held prisoner at the penitentiary here, escaped early yesterday morning, virtually four months to the day after they had been captured at New Lisbon, Ohio.

Following a plan conceived by Capt. T. H. Hines, the group began digging a tunnel from beneath the floor of Hines' cell on Nov. 4, according to a taunting note which the escapees left Warden N. Merion. Even though the cell was inspected daily, no jailor thought to check the carpetbag which hid the hole in the cell floor.

Ever since Gen. Morgan's men had arrived at the Ohio State Penitentiary in Columbus, after being defeated in New Lisbon, Ohio, escaping was their main preoccupation. The obstacles: barred cells, a courtyard guarded by vicious dogs and a surrounding 25-foot-high wall. Remembering *Les Miserables,* Capt. Tom Hines designed a plan.

The men had noticed that the concrete floor of their ground-level cells stayed dry even during the hardest rains, indicating that most likely an air chamber was underneath. Using stolen table knives and working in shifts for 20 days, the men burrowed into that chamber and kept digging until they reached a point below the courtyard. They hid excavated dirt in their mattresses and concealed the hole the few times guards threatened to inspect the cell.

83   **General John Hunt Morgan**

Choosing a rainy night when the dogs would be safely in their kennels, the prisoners crept through the tunnel and scaled the outer wall with a rope made of interwoven sheets.

Once outside, the men scattered. The two leaders, Morgan and Hines, hopped aboard a passenger train to Cincinnati. Fortunately, their prison clothes were not much different from civilian clothes, but to play it safe, Morgan sat next to a uniformed Federal major.

As the train passed the outlying penitentiary, the Union officer reportedly told his traveling companion, "Over there is where they put the Rebel General Morgan for safe-keeping."

"I hope they'll always keep him as safe as he is now," Morgan said slyly.

As the train approached Cincinnati, the two fugitives went to the last car and jumped off as the train slowed down. Within minutes they were on the banks of the Ohio River, there they found someone to row them across to a friendlier shore. In Kentucky they stole horses and headed south toward Tennessee.

In April 1864, Morgan rejoined the Confederate Army and organized a new guerrilla force. Once again he resumed the daring, well-executed raids for which he was known.

In the end, though, the Union had its way. In September 1864, Morgan entered Greenville, Tennessee en route to attack a Union force near Knoxville. Unaware that Federal troops had come into the town during the night, he was taken by surprise, shot and killed.

" Though prison bars,
    My freedom mars,
And glittering bayonets guard me round,
    My Rebel soul
    Scorns such control,
And dwells with friends on Southern ground.
    My heart is light
    And spirits bright,
And Hope, with her enchanting wand,
    Gives visions fair;
    And free as air,
I roam at will in Dixie's Land."

Jeff Thompson, author. Written while imprisoned, August
1863, Gratiot Prison.

84

"Catching a crust," Fort Delaware, August 1863

"**A** number of prisoners from the barracks came into the Fort-yard, this morning, to get water, and to remove some bedding. Several of them crowding into a recess, out of sight of the sentinels, we soon found that the poor fellows were suffering for food, and two or three of our party threw them something to eat. The supply of bread, in all the rooms, seemed tolerably full, and we succeeded in getting a dozen or more loaves, which were thrown out to the sufferers in halves and quarters. It distressed me, to see the eagerness with which they threw up their hands, to catch at every piece. Some who got more than their share, crammed the scraps hastily into their dirty pockets, or hid them in their shirt bosoms. After we had no more to give them, some still waited, anxiously, for a morsel. What a shame to humanity, that these poor men should be subjected to such systematic cruelty, as is said to be practised here! The political prisoners, so far, have "bread enough and to spare," and would gladly divide their surplus with the prisoners of war, but it is contrary to orders; the object being, I suppose, to *starve* the Confederates into taking the oath. I endeavored to encourage them, and every time I threw a piece of bread, exclaimed, "Stand fast, boys! Don't take the oath!" Some of them answered emphatically, "No! No!"

The above two excerpts are from *United States Bonds,* 1874, the personal journal of Isaac W.K. Handy, imprisoned for 15 months at Fort Delaware, Maryland.

In retrospect, the most that can be said for this period of American prison history is that, despite all its mistakes, it was better than a return to the barbarities of capital and corporal punishment. In the face of public indignation to the chaos in early American prisons in this era, it maintained and refined the penitentiary system.

A sudden increase in commitments following the Civil War, and the growing opposition of free labor to prison industries, again brought the prison problem to the public's attention. The federal census reported a total of 19,086 persons in prison in 1860 and 32,901 in 1870—a staggering increase of 72 percent in ten years.

The Box Score on the American Incarceration Rate Begins...

Year	Number of Prisoners	U.S. Population	Prisoners per 100,000 Population
1870	33,000	40 million	83
1860	19,000	31 million	60
1850	7,000	23 million	30
1840	4,000	17 million	24

85 *Pillory and whipping post,*
Joliet Correctional Center, late 1800s

The Reformatory Era

IV

Crime is. . .a moral disease, of which punishment is the remedy. The efficiency of the remedy is a question of social therapeutics, a question of the fitness and the measure of the dose. . .punishment is directed not to the crime but the criminal. . .(in order to reestablish) moral harmony in the soul of the criminal. . .his regeneration—his new birth to have respect for the laws. Hence. . .the supreme aim of prison discipline is the reformation of criminals, not the infliction of vindictive suffering.

Transaction of the National Congress on Prison and Reformatory Discipline, Albany, 1871

The Reformatory System

Drawing class, Sing Sing Prison, New York, 1898

The correctional period from 1870 to 1900 was characterized by the rise of the reformatory system and its program of education and trade training, grades and marks, the indeterminate sentence, and parole. The reformatory system in America owes a great deal to the work of a Scotsman in Australia, Captain Alexander Maconochie, and an Irishman, Sir Walter Crofton. Together they laid the foundation for the development of reformative rather than purely punitive programs for the treatment of criminals.

The first Maconochie innovation was to eliminate the flat sentence, which allowed no hope of release until the full time had been served. Maconochie developed a "mark system," whereby an inmate could earn freedom by hard work and good behavior. This put the burden of release on the inmate. The system had five basic principles:

1. Release was based on the completion of a determined and specified amount of labor.

2. The amount of labor a prisoner had to perform was expressed in a number of "marks" that the prisoner had to earn by improvement of conduct, frugality of living, and habits of industry.

3. Those in prison had to earn

87   *Aging inmates*
Oregon State Penitentiary

everything they received. All sustenance and indulgences were added to their debt of marks.

4. When qualified by good conduct, prisoners would work with six to seven other prisoners, and the whole group would be answerable for the conduct and labor of each member.

5. In the final stage, prisoners, while still obliged to earn their daily tally of marks, were given a proprietary interest in their own labor and were subject to a less rigorous discipline to prepare for release into society.

Maconochie's ideas reached beyond the shores of Australia. His successful use of the indeterminate sentence showed that imprisonment could be used to prepare a prisoner for eventual return to the community.

The "Irish System"

Sir Walter Crofton, an Irish reformer, used this concept in developing what he called the "indeterminate system," also known as the "Irish system." He reasoned that if penitentiaries are places where offenders think about their criminal behavior ("repent"), then there must be a mechanism for releasing the inmate when penitence has been achieved. The indeterminate sentence was believed to be the best mechanism.

The system Crofton devised consisted of a series of stages, each bringing the inmate closer to the free society. The first stage was solitary confinement and dull, monotonous work. The second stage involved assignment to public works and a progression through various grades, each grade shortening the length of stay. The last stage was assignment to an intermediate prison, where the prisoner worked without supervision and moved in and out of the free community.

Prisoners who maintained good conduct and found employment were returned to the community on a conditional pardon or "ticket-of-leave." This ticket could be revoked at any time within the span of the original fixed sentence if a prisoner's conduct did not meet standards established by those supervising the conditional pardon. Crofton's plan was the first to establish a system of conditional liberty in the community.

An Ideal System

Some of the leaders of this period who were familiar with Maconochie's work and with Sir William Crofton's Irish system urged its application in American prisons, and the National Prison Congress of 1870 endorsed these views.

Characteristic public indifference to the plight of prisons in the United States was shattered in 1865, when Enoch Wines, incensed by his visits to several penitentiaries, began a crusade for prison reform. This crusade soared into a dream of a world organization in which outstanding people of all nations would join to plan an ideal prison system.

Wines' mission excited both American and European support, and in the space of a few years, cries for prison reform were resounding around the world.

Guards in the rotunda of Charlestown State Prison, Massachusetts, 1896

Wines believed the first step toward an international congress of prison reformers was the organization of an American association sufficiently representative to call a world meeting. This step was made when primarily American penal reformers and prison administrators met at the National Prison Congress, which convened in Cincinnati in 1870 with 130 delegates from 24 states, Canada, and South America.

View of Cincinnati, Ohio from Mt. Adams, 1872

89

Declaration of Principles

Adopted and Promulgated at the
1870 National Prison Congress
(A Summary)

The Declaration of Principles promoted:

1. Reformation, not vindictive suffering, as the purpose of penal treatment of prisoners.
2. Classifications made on the basis of a mark system, patterned after the Irish system.
3. Rewards for good conduct.
4. Prisoners being made to realize that their destiny is in their own hands.
5. The chief obstacles to prison reform: the political appointment of prison officials and the instability of management.
6. Job training for prison officials.
7. Indeterminate sentences as substitutes for fixed sentences, and removal of the gross disparities and inequities in prison sentences. Also, emphasis on the futility of repeated short sentences.
8. Religion and education as the most important agencies of reformation.
9. Prison discipline that gains the will of prisoners and conserves their self-respect.
10. Making industrious freemen rather than orderly and obedient prisoners as the prison's aim.
11. Full provision for industrial training.
12. Abolishing the system of contract labor in prisons.
13. Small prisons and separate institutions for different types of offenders.
14. Laws striking against the so-called "higher-ups" in crime, as well as against the lesser operatives.
15. Indemnifying prisoners who are later discovered to be innocent.
16. Laws relating to the treatment of insane criminals be revised.
17. More judicious exercise of pardoning power.
18. Establishing a system for the collection of uniform penal statistics.
19. Developing a more adequate prison architecture, providing sufficiently for air and sunlight, as well as for prison hospitals, schoolrooms, etc.
20. Within each state, centralizing prison management.
21. Facilitating the social training of prisoners through proper associations and abolishing the silence rule.
22. Making society at large realize its responsibility for crime conditions.

Among the 40 papers presented were a description by Sir Walter Crofton of the Irish system and a paper by Dr. Wines advocating an international gathering on penal reform. After hearing papers on executive pardon, jails, prison hygiene, and the indeterminate sentence, the Congress adopted the far-reaching Declaration of Principles, which still stands as a progressive document of correctional goals.

Hopes were high when the convention's organizers and prominent leaders throughout the nation signed up as charter members of the National Prison Association (NPA), bringing together officers of the Congress and prominent citizens from throughout the nation.

The NPA sponsored the correctional congresses for several years. The results of the meetings were largely disappointing; however, out of these deliberations emerged the American Prison Association, which later became the American Correctional Association (ACA).

90

William M. F. Round
First Secretary, National Prison Association

The American Correctional Association

For more than a century, the American Correctional Association (ACA) has served as an influential and proactive leader in national and international correctional policies and activities.

ACA was founded in 1870 as the National Prison Association and later called the American Prison Association. At the first organizational meeting in Cincinnati, Ohio, the assembly elected then Ohio governor and future U.S. President Rutherford B. Hayes to be the first president of the Association.

The Declaration of Principles developed at the first meeting in 1870 became the guidelines for corrections in the United States and Europe. At the ACA centennial meeting in 1970, a revised set of principles, reflecting advances in theory and practice, was adopted by the Association. These principles were further revised and updated in January 1982.

At the 1954 Annual Congress of Correction in Philadelphia, Pennsylvania, the name of the American Prison Association was changed to the American Correctional Association reflecting the expanding philosophy of the field and the Association's broadening role.

Working toward a unified voice in correctional policy, the ACA has been actively involved in: developing a national correctional philosophy; designing and implementing standards for correctional services and methods for measuring compliance; and providing publications, training, and technical assistance.

Every year the Association holds a Winter Meeting and, since 1870, a Congress of Correction in August in selected cities across the nation. During these conferences correctional problems and issues covering the entire correctional spectrum are critically examined.

The reform movement, which had gathered itself behind the leadership of Enoch Wines, lost its force by focusing on international corrections, disregarding American correctional problems. Unfortunately, these reformers overestimated the power of their ideas, and the organizations they established were poorly designed to implement their ideas and innovations. Resistance and initial failure nearly destroyed their crusade, leaving to subsequent generations a heritage of idealistic programs set forth in voluminous literature.

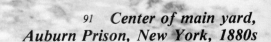

91   Center of main yard, Auburn Prison, New York, 1880s

General Rutherford B. Hayes

Although General Rutherford B. Hayes is most honored and well-known for having served as president of the United States, his achievements as a social reformer and philanthropist are equally significant.

In his obituary of General Hayes, W.M.F. Round wrote, "This good man...did perhaps more than any other man in the country to give stability and character to the Prison Reform movement, to the cause of the education of the colored man, and to a reasonable amelioration of the woes of the Indian."

General Hayes served as an active, reform-minded president of the National Prison Association from 1883 until his death in 1893. In his various speeches and policies, General Hayes took strong, often controversial, positions: He denounced the country's jail system and proposed measures for reforming it; he demanded the separation of young and old inmates; he pleaded for a recognition of the humanity of criminals; he pushed for indeterminate sentences; and he sought better academic and vocational education for offenders.

92

General Rutherford B. Hayes
1822-1893

Elmira Reformatory

One of the reformers, **Zebulon Brockway,** turned his interest from prison association work to concentrate on creating an institution for young offenders where they could receive individual attention and be released when they appeared ready to return to the community.

Overcrowding, which again became evident in the late 1860s, called for additional institutions and it was to these institutions that the new program was applied. The first of these, the Elmira Reformatory in New York, became the model for all that followed.

93

Zebulon R. Brockway
1827-1920

Elmira opened in 1876, with Brockway as superintendent. Offenders from 16 to 30 years of age who were serving their first prison term were sent there. In structure it was similar to the Auburn Prison, with interior cell blocks for solitary confinement at night, and congregate workshops.

The main program differences between the reformatory and the prison were a greater emphasis on reforming youths, more extensive trades training, and an increase in opportunities for academic education. Contract industries were continued, with emphasis on production and profits, except that with the element of training as an excuse, the institution was relieved somewhat of the necessity of being self-supporting.

Elmira Reformatory, Elmira, New York opened in 1876

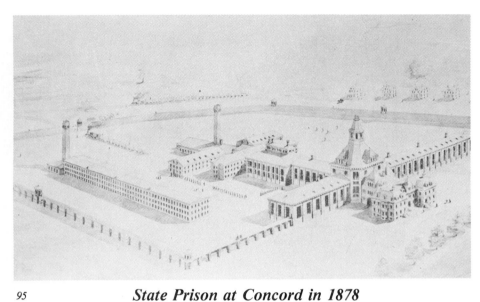

95 ***State Prison at Concord in 1878***
(Now the Massachusetts Reformatory)

96 ***The Ohio Reformatory was designed after the***
Elmira Reformatory in New York

Elmira was copied, in one form or another, by 17 states between 1876 and 1913.

New York (Elmira) 1876
Michigan (Ionia) 1877
Massachusetts (Concord) 1884
Pennsylvania (Huntingdon) . . . 1889
Minnesota (St. Cloud) 1889
Colorado (Buena Vista) 1890

Illinois (Pontiac) 1891
Kansas (Hutchinson) 1895
Ohio (Mansfield) 1896
Indiana (Jeffersonville) 1897
Wisconsin (Green Bay) 1898
New Jersey (Rahway) 1901

Washington (Monroe) 1908-09
Oklahoma (Granite) 1910-11
Maine (S. Windham) 1912-19
Wyoming (Worland) 1912
Nebraska (Lincoln) 1912-13
Connecticut (Cheshire) 1913

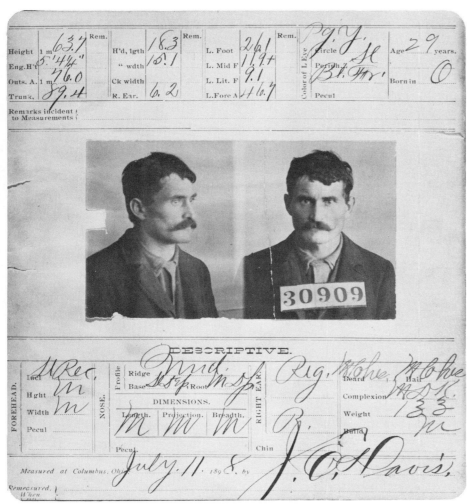

97 **Bertillon System Measurement Card from the Ohio Penitentiary at Columbus**

"Bertillon System for the Identification of Criminals"

The system was introduced in France and other countries by Alphonse Bertillon and adopted in the United States in the late 1880s. Special instruments were used to record height and weight, measurements of the left foot and fingers, head dimensions, etc; full-face and profile photographs were taken.

The Bertillon system of identification and registration of criminals remained in wide use until the advent of the fingerprint as a more positive method of identification.

98 *Tailoring shop, Sing Sing Prison, New York, 1898*

100 *Machine class, Elmira, 1898*

99 *Drafting class, Elmira Reformatory, New York, 1909*

Two outstanding features of the reformatory, however, differed from the typical state prison of this era: (1) Sentences to the reformatory were indeterminate—with fixed maximum terms—and prisoners could be released on parole if their records warranted; and (2) all reformatory inmates were placed into one of three classes based on achievement and conduct. New prisoners were entered in the second grade for the first six months.

Blacksmith course, Elmira, 1898

102   *Sign painting class, Elmira, 1898;*
ceiling frieze decorating also taught

They were then either demoted to the third grade for bad conduct or promoted to the first grade as they earned their "marks." Only prisoners who were in the first grade were eligible for parole. Later, when contracts were outlawed, it appeared there would be no industrial programs. Military drill and organized athletics were introduced as substitutes and these became regular features of the reformatory program. Within the next 25 years, reformatories were organized in 12 states.

The reformatory movement reached its peak in 1910. To be sure, a few more Elmira-patterned reformatories were established during the next two decades, but on the whole the program had reached its zenith.

103 *Prisoner regiment passing in review, Elmira, 1880s*

1900 view of a prison classroom

The reformatory movement came at a time when public education was rapidly developing as the social reformers' answer to many problems. Thus, it is not surprising that education also became the answer to crime.

The education program Zebulon Brockway established at Elmira was a valuable contribution to American penology. Excluding the Sabbath schools of the preceding period, this was the first attempt to organize a program of positive reformation on a scale that would include all inmates of a correctional institution.

However, an educational program such as this required a high quality of leadership and staff to maintain it. The need for specialists to work with socially maladjusted students also became evident but was not recognized by American society. Administrators continued to assign to reformatories the same type of personnel who had been assigned to prisons in the past, and a few underpaid and overworked instructors.

105   *Corn husking outdoors*

106   *Caning room, 1890*

Weaving looms. Sturdy hickory cloth was made into inmates' clothing, 1902

The Laundry at Elmira, 1906

Reformatories became junior prisons in which education and trade training were available for some inmates, while the majority continued to carry on the usual institutional and industrial routine and learn other, less desirable skills from peers.

The grading system was too complicated to maintain for a staff that tended to change with each new political administration. The tendency was to put everyone who behaved into the first grade, leaving only a few in the second grade, and those actually under punishment in the third grade. The old prison discipline, which placed emphasis on being a good prisoner, still dominated.

By 1869, "good time" laws, which automatically reduced prison sentences for good work and good behavior, were passed in 23 states. During the period from 1870 to 1900, all the prisons built were of the Auburn type, the only improvements being the introduction of ventilating systems and steel cells with plumbing and running water in each. Still, 77 prisons used the bucket system of waste disposal as late as the 1930s.

Most of these prisons had some kind of rudimentary education program, including a prison library. Official chaplains regularly conducted religious services on Sundays. Except as modified by the indeterminate sentence and parole and the abandonment of the silent system, the old system of prison discipline and industrial production continued to govern.

109

Western Penitentiary, Pittsburgh, Pennsylvania 1892. Auburn-style inside cell blocks in long flanking cell houses.

The Leasing System

The most decisive event in the history of southern penology was the Civil War.

According to historian Mark T. Carlton and others, after 1865, the status of half the population—the slaves—was changed, with a devastating effect on the correctional system. Instead of being punished on plantations, former slaves were jammed into overcrowded, dilapidated correctional facilities. Although nothing was done to alleviate these conditions, the cost of feeding, clothing, and guarding so many extra prisoners alone was a financial undertaking that the Southern states' meager economies were not prepared to handle.

Southern legislatures were attracted to the leasing system because it offered them the possibility of not only avoiding the financial embarrassment of supporting convicts, but also of deriving a revenue from the transaction.

110

Portable jail wagons on laundry day, Georgia

Private contractors were as eager to obtain cheap prisoner labor for a variety of projects ranging from levee and railroad construction to plantation work as Southern legislatures were to accommodate them. By 1870, arrangements for leasing were made and for more than a generation in some states, the convict lease system remained the dominant feature of southern penology. The War Between the States had virtually wiped out the beginnings of the penitentiary system in several southern states. Some found a solution in leasing out their entire prison population. Others maintained central prisons, but leased the majority of their prisoners to private companies. Still others retained the contract system. Thus, while northern and western states were abandoning the lease and contract systems in favor of piece-price, state-account, and state-use systems, the border states continued to be subservient to contractors.

A formal pose, Pitt County, North Carolina

112   *Mobile cage provided transportation and sleeping quarters for 30 convicts*

In the 19th century there were two basic patterns of convict leasing. Under the contract system state officials were responsible for feeding, clothing, and guarding the convicts, who worked within the prison structure. Lessees hired only convict labor, not the convicts themselves. South Carolina, Texas, and Virginia had adopted this system by the 1880s. All other southern states, as well as Nebraska and the New Mexico Territory, used the lease system, which differed from the contract system in that lessees could work convicts outside of the prison structure.

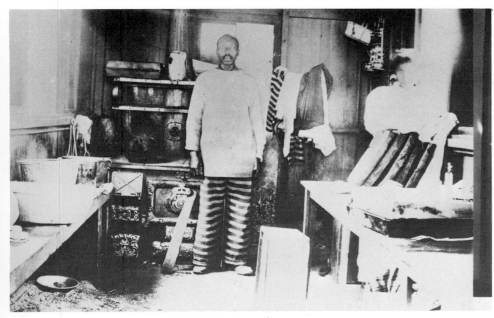

Prison wagon kitchen

Interior of bunk wagon

As most blacks were experienced agricultural workers, the majority were eventually employed by the lessees as cotton and fruit pickers, sugar cane cutters, and vegetable gardeners. Out of these situations arose the penal farm, an institution uniquely southern, which in at least Louisiana, still serves as the center of correctional operations.

Unfortunately, the lessees' goal of making money for themselves and for the state was incompatible with carrying out programs of reform and rehabilitation. The latter aim was cast away in favor of profits. Humane treatment of prisoners also took a back seat to profit making. Under these circumstances, it is understandable that although prison reform made headway elsewhere in the United States during the late 19th century, in the South no comparable progress was evident for decades to come.

In the development of American prisons, southern states did not conform to the general pattern set by Auburn or the reformatory. In part, this was due to special problems related to former slaves and the essentially agrarian society of the South.

Camp with jail on wheels

The Reformatory Period (1870-1900) will be remembered in penal history for two things: the indeterminate sentence and parole, and the introduction to a positive reform program through education. The former provided a powerful incentive that took the place of the old prison discipline following the breakdown of noncommunication as the principal rule in the Auburn and Pennsylvania systems. The latter, although it did not succeed because it could not rise above staffing constraints, modified the thinking and recognized objectives of the Auburn prison enough to make its severe discipline more tolerable.

The Box Score on the American Incarceration Rate continues...

Year	Number of Prisoners	U.S. Population	Prisoners per 100,000 Population
1900	57,000	76 million	75
1890	45,000	63 million	71
1870	33,000	40 million	83
1860	19,000	31 million	60
1850	7,000	23 million	30
1840	4,000	17 million	24

116 **Convicts chained together, Charlotte, NC**

Through World War I

V

Exploitation of their labor has embittered the hearts of prisoners and they have come out of prison more vindictive and more ready to injure society than they were when first placed within prison walls.

Louis N. Robinson, 1921
Penology in the United States

The Industrial Period

The first quarter of the 20th century is frequently called the "industrial period" in American penal history.

Factory prisons, producing a broad range of finished products for military, public, and state government consumption, flourished in the North, Midwest, and West.

○ ANGOLA ○ 1900

TAG PLANT

117 ○ LOUISIANA ○

118   *Contract industrial system, Joliet, Illinois, c. 1900*

With a new emphasis on group labor, American correctional practice underwent several significant changes. Silence was no longer enforced and there was less emphasis on religious instruction, education, and trade training. In addition, greater emphasis was placed on using parole as an incentive for good behavior rather than relying solely on corporal punishment and other negative sanctions.

119

The brickyard at Kansas State Penitentiary, where, for over 75 years, inmates fired the kilns on the banks of the Missouri River to make bricks for several state and county institutions. The kilns were cooled off in the 1960s and dismantled. Nearby was the entrance to the deep shaft coal mines that ran under the river. A state regulation provided that inmates earn two days off their sentences for every day served in the mines.

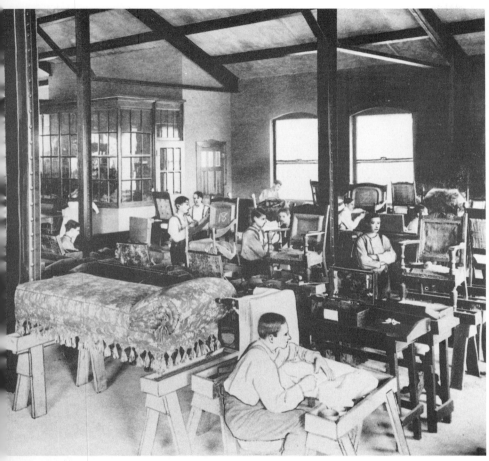

120   *Upholstery Class, Elmira, New York, 1909*

121   *Cement block shed, Riker's Island, New York*

122 *Hand looms to produce toweling,*
Clinton Prison, New York

123

Contract Industrial System

Canning plant showing steam pressure kettles. Louisiana State Prison, Angola, top

Blacksmith Shop, Connecticut Reformatory, Cheshire, Connecticut, bottom left

Wicker shop at the Joliet Correctional Center, 1920s bottom right

124

125

Prison Farms

Around the turn of the century, many states began to move away from the leasing system to one that relied on inmate labor to work large state-owned prison farms. Farm labor, often "stoop work" involving picking, weeding, harvesting, and other arduous chores, was at least preferable to some of the brutalities that had occurred under the leasing system.

127

Grading a farm road, Indiana State Farm, 1915

126

128

Joliet Correctional Center, early 1900s

The underlying motive for establishing large prison farms was the same as for the north's industrial prisons: profit for the state.

131   *Tending the hogs*

130   *Roll call, Indiana State Prison Farm, Greencastle*

132   *In the potato bin, New Jersey State Prison Farm, Bordentown*

Extensive tracts of land were cultivated on state prison farms. In 1921, South Carolina had 4,168 acres under cultivation; Louisiana, 15,600 acres; Florida, 17,000 acres; Mississippi, 28,750 acres; and Texas, 73,461 acres.

104

133   *Plowing time*

Down on the old prison farm, complete with a brace of oxen. By 1973, many prisons began phasing out their farm operations for two reasons: (1) Farm jobs were hard to obtain for parolees, and (2) state-produced food was more expensive than bid-purchased food from private industry.

Windsor Prison, Vermont

While prisoners in the north grew pale and anemic from prolonged confinement in huge institutional structures, the situation was quite different in the South. The practice of leasing convicted offenders to private contractors to perform different types of hard labor continued into the 1920s in several states.

This system had been the subject of considerable abuse in many states. Offenders were chained together in "gangs," while dogs and mounted armed guards provided security. Because guards were frequently fined or fired for escapes, scores of fugitives were shot every year.

Prison labor was used extensively in the road-building process in many states.

135   *Breaking stone for a highway, 1916*

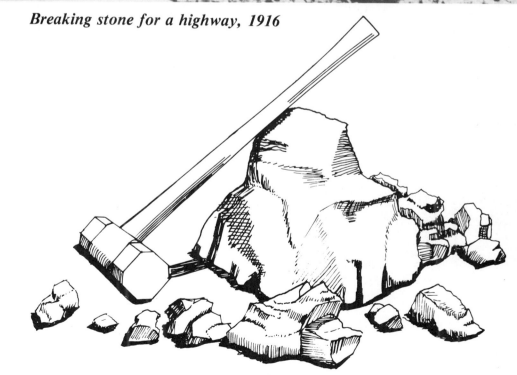

Building Yosemite Highway, California

137 **More Yosemite construction**

Rock quarry, State Prison at Folsom, Represa, California

Building a Railroad

Many miles of track were laid and maintained by inmate labor.

A half mile of standard railroad, constructed at a cost of $6,000 using inmate labor, was an estimated savings of $5,000 for the state

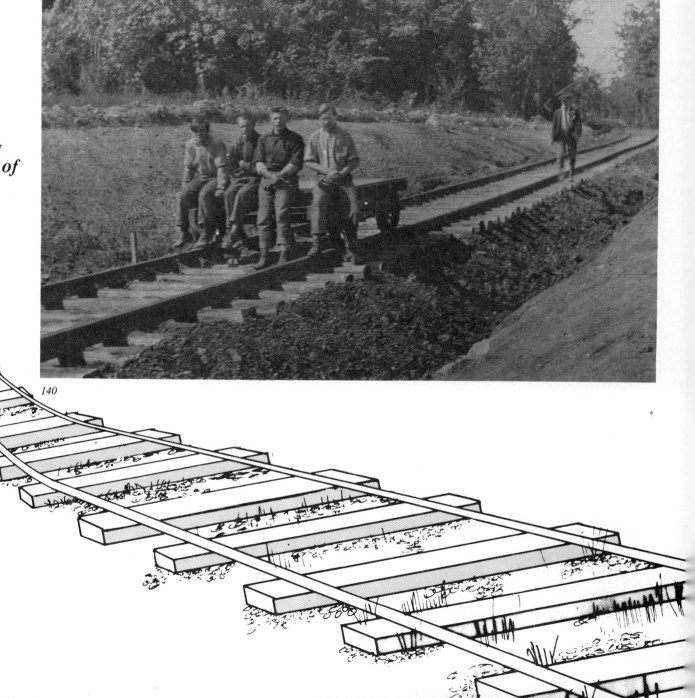

140

139

141

A road engine of the 1920s picking up the prison pullmans in which large numbers of prisoners were transferred to other institutions. The railroads gave these prison trains right-of-way over all else and schedules were kept secret throughout the moves. Railroad special agents accompanied prison guards during the trip.

111

Building a Prison

142 **Wall construction at a penitentiary**

Men at work building their own prison step by step

143

144

145 ***Installing plumbing in Cell House "B"
Illinois State Penitentiary, 1931***

113

Prison Camps

The use of prison camps or colonies served the needs of state and county projects such as road building, levee construction, agricultural needs, and railroad construction.

Camps were originally established in the early 1920s to relieve overcrowding and to provide profitable outdoor work that would aid in rehabilitation. Residents were on their honor to abide by camp regulations and guarding and locking up was considered unnecessary.

In California, the penalty for escaping from a road camp was up to five years in San Quentin State Prison.

146 *Kitchen, Lewis County Jail Camp, New York*

147 *Camp office*

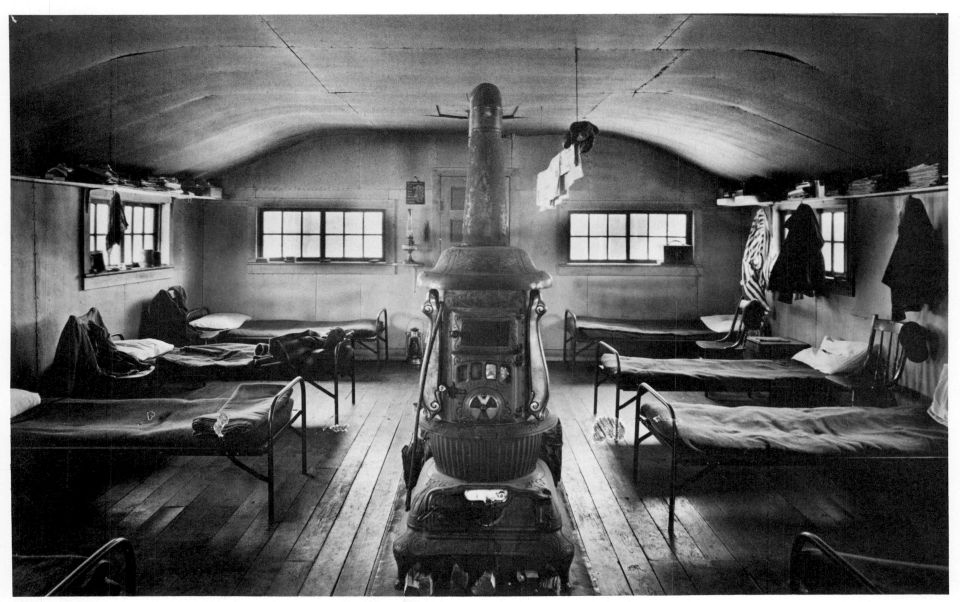

Sleeping quarters, Lewis County Jail Camp

149 ***When road work was finished in a district, camps were completely dismantled. The buildings, built in***
sections, were taken apart and reassembled at a new location. (California Detention Camp)

116

150

Camp Dormitory

151

152 **The original "Saturday Night Special"**

Dining room, Angola, Louisiana work camp

The Warden...

...his family

154

155 *Duty as the warden's driver was one of the most sought-after jobs for inmates*

156

157

158

. . .and his staff

Off duty guards, top left
Oregon State Penitentiary,
top right
A new motorbike for a member
of staff, right

159

160   *Making do*

161   *Joliet Penitentiary*

Parades, bunting-draped walls, entertainment, and speeches

162   *Marching Band*

The fourth of July in the yard

163

Joliet Penitentiary

164 **Joliet Penitentiary**

165 *Hand-pulled fire engine with inmate crew at a midwestern penitentiary*

166 *Horse-drawn trolley to Joliet Penitentiary*

167

O. Henry (1862-1910)

O. Henry was the pen name of William Sydney Porter, who began his writings as an inmate of the Ohio Penitentiary at Columbus. A master of the short story, he wrote in a simple style in the language of the man on the street. His sympathy for human weaknesses and the naturalness of his characters continue to make his stories interesting. He published about 14 volumes of stories reflecting his own experiences and those of his associates. Some of his best known story characters were criminals and soldiers of fortune. His works include "The Gift of the Magi," "Waifs and Strays," "Cabbages and Kings," and "The Gentle Crafter."

Prison populations in the United States more than doubled in the 35 years between 1890 and 1925. The growth was relatively slow during the first two decades of the century. After 1920, prison populations began a period of rapid growth that was not interrupted until the outbreak of World War II. In 1925 there were approximately 93,000 men and women in American prisons, penitentiaries, and adult reformatories.

Contributing Factors

An increase in unemployment following World War I probably contributed to the growing crime rate during the early 1920s. New laws and enforcement of prohibition also contributed. Passage of the Volstead Act in 1918 made the manufacture and sale of alcohol a federal crime. Bootlegging soon became epidemic and helped to illegally fill the unemployment void for thousands.

168 The way it was

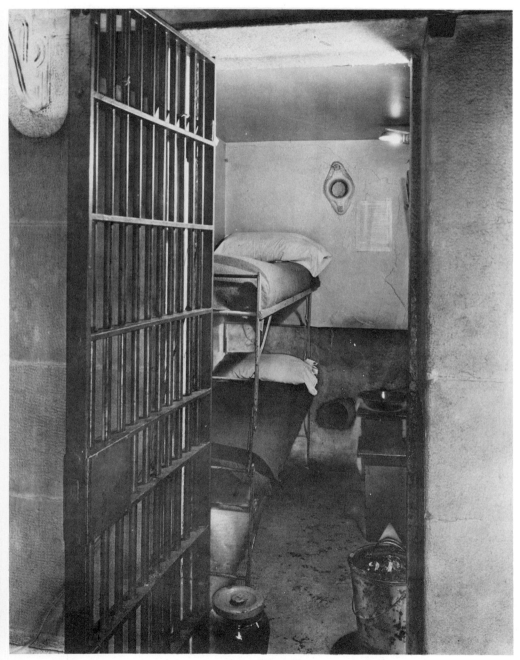

An old cell

In 1919, the National Motor Vehicle Theft Act made interstate transportation of stolen vehicles a federal offense and provided for the arrest, prosecution, and incarceration of interstate auto thieves. Under this Act the U.S. government was authorized to prosecute offenders in either the state where the theft occurred or in the state where they were arrested. Upon conviction, the offender could be sentenced to a state or federal penal institution.

The Act was rigorously enforced after the creation of the Federal Bureau of Investigation (FBI) in 1924. This national police force had agents in every state and enforced federal laws against kidnapping, bank robbery, and interstate transportation of stolen vehicles. Unemployment, increased mobility, new laws, and improved enforcement all contributed to the rapid growth in the number of Americans in penal institutions.

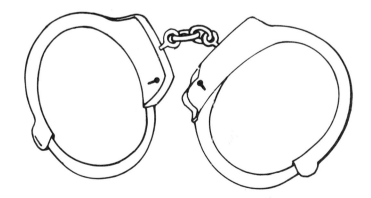

Rising prison populations necessitated additional prison construction. Between 1900 and 1925, 31 major prisons and seven reformatories for adults were built in the United States—all but two are still in use today. In general, these prisons were large fortress-like structures holding over 1,000 and in some cases 2,000 inmates. Most were the Auburn type with multiple tiers of small, steel interior cells designed for a single inmate. The cells were furnished with open plumbing and running water. Some, built during this period, such as Union Correctional Institute in Raiford, Florida, were described as being "as cold and hard and abnormal as the prisoners whom they were intended to persuade toward better things."

The seven reformatories built between 1900 and 1919 were the last gasp of the declining reformatory movement that had begun in 1870. In 1920, there were 29 reformatories for adults in the United States, 18 for men and 11 for women. A number of prisons originally designed as reformatories still bear that name, such as Washington State Reformatory at Monroe, built in 1908. Others, such as the Reformatory at Rahway, New Jersey, opened in 1901, have subsequently been redesignated as state prisons.

Despite the construction boom of this period, overcrowding and lack of adequate programs and facilities continued as serious problems in American prisons—problems that are still evident today.

170

Florida State Prison, Raiford

Separate confinement, that is, one person per cell, has been the goal of virtually every prison system, including the original Auburn and Pennsylvania models. Almost all prison cells were designed for single inhabitants with dining, work, education, and recreation facilities based on the number of cells.

Meeting of inmate delegates of Mutual Welfare League for Prisoners, Auburn, New York, 1914, below

Delivering the mail, Washington State Penitentiary, right

171

172

Then as now, state legislatures were reluctant to provide the capital and operating budgets to accommodate the ever-increasing numbers of prisoners. Serious overcrowding was the rule in American corrections. Two, three, and even four inmates were forced to live together in small (perhaps six feet by eight feet) cells designed for one person. In addition to psychological and social difficulties, this situation also created serious medical problems. The "Great White Plague," tuberculosis, made its home in prisons. More than life sentences or capital punishment, this dread disease prevented many inmates from ever returning to society.

Inadequate Care

Most prisons also lacked proper medical facilities. In the 1918 *Annual Report* of the New Jersey prison system, it was noted that it was not possible to segregate syphilitic and tubercular prisoners from the general prison population. In the same year, an administrator in the Wisconsin state prison system complained that insane and mentally ill prisoners were kept in solitary confinement because there was nowhere else to place them.

130

173 *Sanitation inspector with institution official at Massachusetts institution. Caption reads, "Windows provide ample ventilation, reducing chances for tuberculosis."*

Buckets used as chamber pots, also called "honey pots," were emptied into a sewer trough. "About one thousand men and boys must stand in line twice daily waiting their turn to empty their chamber pots after using them in their cells for about 12 hours."

Old Penitentiary for Males, Welfare Island, New York, 1924

If medical facilities were inadequate, education and literacy programs were also receiving only token attention. Nearly every prison and reformatory had at least one chaplain who, in addition to Sunday sermons, was also responsible for educational and recreational programs.

Many prison education programs operated only in the evenings during winter months. Children's primers were used for educating illiterate adults. In a survey of 110 prisons and reformatories conducted in 1927-28, it was found that most prisons offered almost nothing in the way of general education programs, much less in vocational education.

176 Youths and old men shared this penitentiary classroom. Subjects ranged from butterflies to Abe Lincoln.

Cell 38, Sing Sing Penitentiary, New York

Oscar Wilde (1854-1900)

On May 27, 1895, Oscar Wilde was imprisoned for perjury for two years in Her Majesty's Prison in Reading, England. After his release in February of 1898, he wrote a 110 stanza poem entitled *The Ballad of Reading Gaol*. Several poignant excerpts are cited below:

> The vilest deeds like poison weeds,
> Bloom well in prison-air;
> It is only what is good in Man
> That wastes and withers there:
> Pale Anguish keeps the heavy gate,
> And the Warder is Despair.
>
> For they starve the little frightened child
> Till it weeps both night and day:
> And they scourge the weak, and flog the fool,
> And gibe the old and grey,
> And some grow mad, and all grow bad,
> And none a word may say.
>
> Each narrow cell in which we dwell
> Is a foul and dark latrine,
> And the fetid breath of living Death
> Chokes up each grated screen,
> And all, but Lust, is turned to dust
> In Humanity's machine.
>
> The brackish water that we drink
> Creeps with a loathsome slime,
> And the bitter bread they weigh in scales
> Is full of chalk and lime,
> And Sleep will not lie down, but walks
> Wild-eyed, and cries to Time.

One of Oscar Wilde's most famous letters from *De Profundis*, was written to Lord Alfred Douglas while Wilde was jailed in Reading Gaol. One passage of the very long letter depicts prison life in 1895 as follows:

" But we who live in prison, and in whose lives there is no event but sorrow, have to measure time by throbs of pain, and the record of bitter moments. We have nothing else to think of. Suffering—curious as it may sound to you—is the means by which we exist, because it is the only means by which we become conscious of existing; and the remembrance of suffering in the past is necessary to us as the warrant, the evidence of our continued identity."

PUBLIC SCRUTINY OF PRISON POLICY AND CONDITIONS

in any part of the United States was, as always, minimal. Most prisons were located in remote rural areas far from the urban settings that provided most of the prisoners. The "out of sight, out of mind" principle still prevailed. Facing overcrowded facilities with insufficient resources and staff and primitive physical plants, prison administrators emphasized control and conformity rather than modifying prisoners' behavior.

134

*178 **Joliet Correctional Center, Illinois***

Correctional administrators were judged by their ability to pump goods out and keep prisoners in. Inmate reformation became an unplanned by-product of prison industry. Prison work, whether agricultural or industrial, was primarily seen as supporting control by keeping prisoners busy and providing income to the state. Teaching useful skills was purely coincidental.

179

One form of punishment used during the 1920s was to stand still for many hours on the lines on the floor. Joliet Correctional Center, Disciplinary Building

135

STAR OF HOPE

Established 1899

Circulation 9,000

Vol. XVIII   No. 6

Opportunity

THERE'S a chance for the fellow who tries;
There's a chance for the fellow who dreams;
There's many a chance if you look at the skies,
But chance is not what it seems.

Chance is never a dream of swift wealth,
Or vision of sudden found gains.
Chance, as you call it rests in self
And the taking of infinite pains.

Chance as you'll find it comes alone,
It wings but once to your door—
'Tis an arrow that strikes while many unknown
Have missed the target before.
                            Sing Sing No. 65368.

EDITORIAL STAFF

EDITOR-IN-CHIEF
HENRY LEVERAGE (Sing Sing No. 65368)

ASSOCIATE EDITORS

JOHN L. JOHNSON (Sing Sing No. 66062)   THOMAS A. REID (Sing Sing No. 64846)

The *Star of Hope* is published monthly at 354 Hunter Street, Ossining, N. Y., for and by the inmates of New York's five State Prisons. Subscription price $2.50, subject to the laws of the State of New York. Entered as Second Class mail matter, June 6, 1904, at the Post Office at Ossining, N. Y.

180 *"Escapees, when returned, have a chain riveted to one of their legs. The chain is five feet long and weighs 20 pounds. It becomes a part of the man both day and night." Sing Sing Penitentiary, 1916*

Iron "picks," riveted above the ankles, hobbled the prisoners, preventing them from running away. The burlap wrapping was to prevent chafing.

AMERICAN PRISON POLICY BETWEEN 1900 AND 1925 CAN BE SUMMED UP IN THREE WORDS: CUSTODIAL, PUNITIVE, AND PRODUCTIVE. It relied on total control, punishment, and hard labor. Aside from greater emphasis on production and profit and less emphasis on classification, education, and moral instruction, correctional practices in American prisons in the early 20th century did not differ greatly from practices in the early 19th century.

"THE OLD PRISON DISCIPLINE"

CUSTODIAL, PUNITIVE, AND PRODUCTIVE practices, sometimes called the "old prison discipline," have been outlined by Howard B. Gill.*

Elam Lynds, the warden of Auburn Prison around 1825, established a discipline recognized by prison workers 100 years later. Lynds' discipline assumed that criminals could not be reformed until their spirits were broken. This assumption, like the discipline, prevailed throughout the United States for a century.

According to Gill, prison discipline stood for the following:

Hard Labor—Ranging from "making little ones out of big ones" and carrying cannon shot from one end of the prison yard to the other, to constructive prison industries.

Deprivation—Of everything except the requisites for a spartan existence and religious instruction.

Monotony—Essentially no variation in diet and daily routine.

Uniformity—Rigidly consistent treatment of prisoners.

Mass Movement—Individuality was squashed through mass living in cell blocks, mass eating, mass recreation, even mass bathing.

Degradation—To complete the loss of identity, prisoners were housed in monkey cages, dressed in shabby, nondescript clothing, and denied courteous contacts with guards.

Subservience—To rules, rules, rules!

Corporal Punishment—Among the uses of force were the paddle, the whip, the sweat box, and the famous boot.

Noncommunication—Absolute silence or solitary confinement, without relief from letters, visits, or other contacts.

Recreation—At first none; later a daily hour in the yard.

No Responsibility—Prisoners were denied every social, civic, domestic, economic, and even personal responsibility.

Isolation—Often 16 hours a day, thereby increasing prisoners' egocentricity.

No "Fraternization" with the Guards—This rule prevented any attempts to solve problems through staff-inmate contacts.

---

*Howard B. Gill. "A New Prison Discipline: Implementing the Declaration of Principles of 1870," *Federal Probation*, Vol. 34, No. 2 (June 1970), pp. 29-30.

Denying basic human needs, the prison discipline before 1925 fostered a host of pathologies including guilt, inferiority, inadequacy, self-absorption, apathy, and despair.

182 *Great Meadow Prison, Comstock, New York*

CAPITAL PUNISHMENT

The most severe and hotly debated sanction used in the United States is capital punishment, or execution, in the name of the state

183 *Lynching of Frank McManus, April 28, 1882. McManus was hanged by a group of well-respected citizens seeking justice against an outrageous crime. Condoned by the entire community, the hanging inspired publication of a small book entitled "The Minneapolis Tragedy: Full Account of the Crime of a Fiend, of Frank McManus and the Swift Retribution of an Outraged Community."*

Electric chair, Ohio State Penitentiary

Applied extensively throughout American history, capital punishment has usually been reserved for the most heinous criminal offenses, particularly murder and rape. Between 1930 and 1965, over 3,800 offenders were executed in the United States.

The means by which capital punishment has been carried out have varied much more than the crimes for which this punishment has been applied. In tribal societies, the death penalty often took the form of banishment. With the development of modern society, methods of capital punishment "advanced"—the condemned have been hanged, drowned, crushed, beheaded, electrocuted, smothered, gassed, shot, or, more recently, injected with lethal drugs.

Early executions were almost always public spectacles, with the hope that they would serve as a warning and deterrent to others and provide the only real assurance that brutal criminals would not continue to threaten society. Current forms of execution are less cruel, more private, and perhaps more humane, but controversy still centers on the extent of the death penalty's deterrent value.

185

142

186 *Gas chamber*
California State Prison
San Quentin

IN RECENT YEARS the deterrent effect and the constitutionality of the death penalty have been issues of major concern to judges and social scientists in the United States. Critics of capital punishment have argued that the sentence has usually been imposed in a racially biased manner. A disproportionate number of blacks (53.5 percent of all executions) have received the death sentence and been executed. Eighty percent of those executed for rape between 1930 and 1977 were black.

187 *Scaffolding for hanging, Oregon State Penitentiary*

CRUEL AND UNUSUAL PUNISHMENT

In 1972, the Supreme Court, objecting to the arbitrary and capricious manner in which the death penalty was being imposed, ruled in *Furman v. Georgia* that the discretionary imposition of the death penalty was cruel and unusual punishment under the 8th and 14th amendments of the Constitution.

Considerable research, including studies by Robert Dann, Karl Schuessler, Thorsten Sellin, and Walter Reckless, indicated that executing convicted criminals has relatively little deterrent effect. One of the few studies in which capital punishment was found to have a deterrent effect was a 1975 study by Isaac Ehrlich at the University of Chicago. However, William Bowers and Glenn Pierce repeated the study and found punishment to be no more effective as a deterrent to crime than life imprisonment.

Recent experience in Canada offers new hope for the abolitionists. Canada abolished the death penalty in 1976 and, from 1975 to 1979, the incidence of murder *decreased* by 18 percent—from 2.8 murders per 100,000 population to 2.3.

Nevertheless, the death row population in the United States swelled to 1,168 persons in early 1983.

188   *Texas' needle: the first execution by injection, December 7, 1982*

*189 **Watch tower of the Indiana Reformatory
in Pendleton, 1938***

Post World War I

VI

Society has become more and more aware that the mere incarceration of criminals does not solve the crime problem. It has become increasingly evident that the solution does not lie in depriving men of freedom or social privileges, or in punishment per se. Intelligent treatment of the problem demands that the agents whom society has designated to protect it from the onslaughts of criminals be aware of all the conditions—economic, social and personal— which have been the cause of the criminal and anti-social tendencies of the prisoner.

EDWARD P. MULROONEY
Commissioner of Correction
State of New York

Foreword in Walter M. Wallack, THE TRAINING OF PRISON GUARDS IN THE STATE OF NEW YORK, N.Y. Teachers College, Columbia University, 1938, p. v.

POST WORLD WAR I

THE POST-WORLD WAR I
THROUGH WORLD WAR II ERA
(1926-1950) witnessed profound and
fundamental changes in American
prisons' purpose and nature.

The gradual disappearance of the striped
uniform and the lockstep were early signs
of change. More significantly, however,
was the subtle shift in the conception of
the criminal as sinner to the criminal as
sick, needing specialized diagnosis and
treatment. During this period, the prison
became the correctional center, in name
if not in fact.

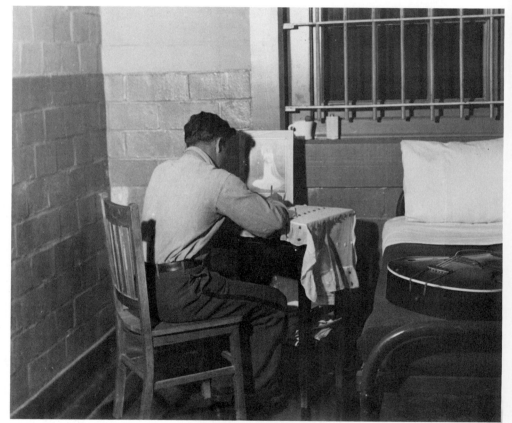

190

Prison cell, 1939

Florida State Prison, 1938

150

192   Mess hall, California State Prison at San Quentin, 1948

193

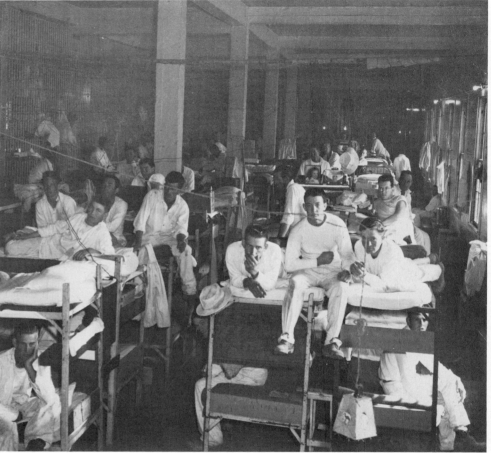

194   *Housing area, Texas Department of Corrections, 1940s*

195   *Unidentified American city jail, top*

2:30 a.m.   A view of the Fresno County Jail holdover tank, 1938, bottom

The single most powerful factor affecting correctional systems during this period was overcrowding resulting from profound changes in the social order and economy of the nation during the Depression, World War II, and the postwar period.

196　*Main yard, Washington State Penitentiary, 1930s*

The marked decline in foreign immigration after World War I resulted in the need for America's heavy industries to turn to the South to fill the constant demand for unskilled labor.

197　　　　　　　　*Auburn Prison, New York, 1927*

198 *Marching in columns of two
center of main yard
Auburn Prison, New York
early 1900s*

A new migration of blacks to the north brought a rapid increase in their numbers in prison populations. Concurrently, mounting crime rates in the affluent 1920s, the growth of interstate regulatory laws, and, most significantly, Prohibition, dramatically increased the number of state and federal offenders.

199 **Steel box provides security in a wooden building**

200 *Foundry,*
Indiana Reformatory,
Pendleton, 1938

Responding to this situation, the Hoover administration created the U.S. Bureau of Prisons, which from its early years has been influential in shaping the development of American prisons.

UNITED STATES PENITENTIARY
ALCATRAZ
California

201   *United States Penitentiary, Alcatraz. Long used as an Army prison, the Bureau of Prisons took over Alcatraz Island in 1934. Extensive changes and additions to the original building were eventually made.*

UNITED STATES INDUSTRIAL REFORMATORY - CHILLICOTHE OHIO
TEACHING SELF RELIANCE AND SELF RESPECT

202

203 *Federal Correctional Institution, La Tuna, Texas*

204 *Chair factory under construction, U.S. Reformatory, Chillicothe, Ohio*

The economic hardships of the Depression led 33 states to pass laws in the 1930s prohibiting the sale of convict-made products on the open market. Fortunately, Eleanor Roosevelt interceded to secure the President's backing in creating the U.S. Bureau of Prisons' prison industries as an independent corporation, ensuring its survival as a prisoner training and government-use production program. The National Recovery Act became a catalyst for state programs to implement measures to relieve the pressures of overcrowding and inmate idleness.

205   *Blacksmith Shop, Illinois State Penitentiary, Pontiac*

206   *Tailor shop, Folsom State Prison, California*

159

207 *Broom-making, Indiana Reformatory, Pendleton, 1938*

208   Inmate dining room, seating capacity 2,000, Stateville, Illinois

210 *Newly arrived residents*

209 *Riker's Island, New York*

"Scow tied up to the pier of the unloading plant on New York's Riker's Island ready for unloading, 1924. Prisoners are profitably employed in trimming the heaped rubbish, separating wood for fuel from other materials with profit for the city."

211

Fear of crime and increasing pressure for determinate sentencing were reflected in the increasing number of prisoners in the United States. However, at the same time, the thesis stressing social causes of crime gained acceptance over the traditional definition of the criminal as a "sinner." Imprisonment as a justifiable expression of public moral indignation declined, at least in the ranks of influential correctional professionals.

A number of extremely serious riots and the horrible tragedy of the Ohio State Prison fire, involving 322 deaths, resulted in dramatic efforts to find new ways to house and work inmates. New and better systems for classifying inmates and a variety of appropriate physical plant designs emerged. Once again state prisons turned to the development of honor farms, road crews, forestry camps, prison farms, prison plantations, and more expedient systems for traditional parole release programs to ease overcrowding.

212
Cleaning up debris following the fire at Ohio State Prison April 1930

WOMEN IN PRISONS

AMERICAN WOMEN FIRST BECAME ZEALOUSLY INVOLVED IN CORRECTIONAL REFORM IN THE 19TH CENTURY, when the status and role of women were changing rapidly. Both middle- and upper-class ladies devoted to the "cult of true womanhood" and educated women entering the male world of employment supported reforms for "fallen" women. Foremost was the belief that female offenders could be rehabilitated only if they were isolated from the corrupting influence of men, by keeping them in prisons for female offenders only, with female staff.

Previously, female offenders had been considered beyond rehabilitation. In straying from the "proper" womanly role, female offenders were committing acts considered only within the capability of evil men. Thus, women were confined in wings, rooms, and attics of men's penitentiaries, separated from male inmates but supervised by male correctional officers.

213 ***Women's Prison corridor, New York Tombs***

Women's Prison, Joliet, Illinois, early 1900s

Women—regardless of their offense, age, background, health, or maternal status—lived together in one area. To be a woman in prison was "worse than death," Chaplain B.C. Smith of Auburn Penitentiary in New York said in 1832. Only a few individuals, with religious motivations, attempted to help female offenders.

215   *Elizabeth Gurney Fry*

Elizabeth Gurney Fry, an English Quaker, is credited with establishing the theoretical and practical bases for women's corrections. Working in the women's section of Newgate Prison in London in the early decades of the 19th century, Fry demonstrated that even the most depraved women were redeemable. Her success prompted substantial change in penal reformers' attitudes toward female offenders.

Fry recommended a program that has since become central to women's corrections. First, she advocated separating female inmates from male inmates and male correctional officers by placing them in separate facilities—supervised and staffed only by women. Instead of physical punishment, she supported humane treatment. Fry urged that, using volunteers and community resources, women be placed in treatment groups and programs for cleanliness, work, education, and religious instruction.

The first American experimental implementation of Fry's proposal was the House of Refuge established in New York City in 1825, in response to the problems of homeless and delinquent juveniles. A separate building for female juvenile delinquents was opened.

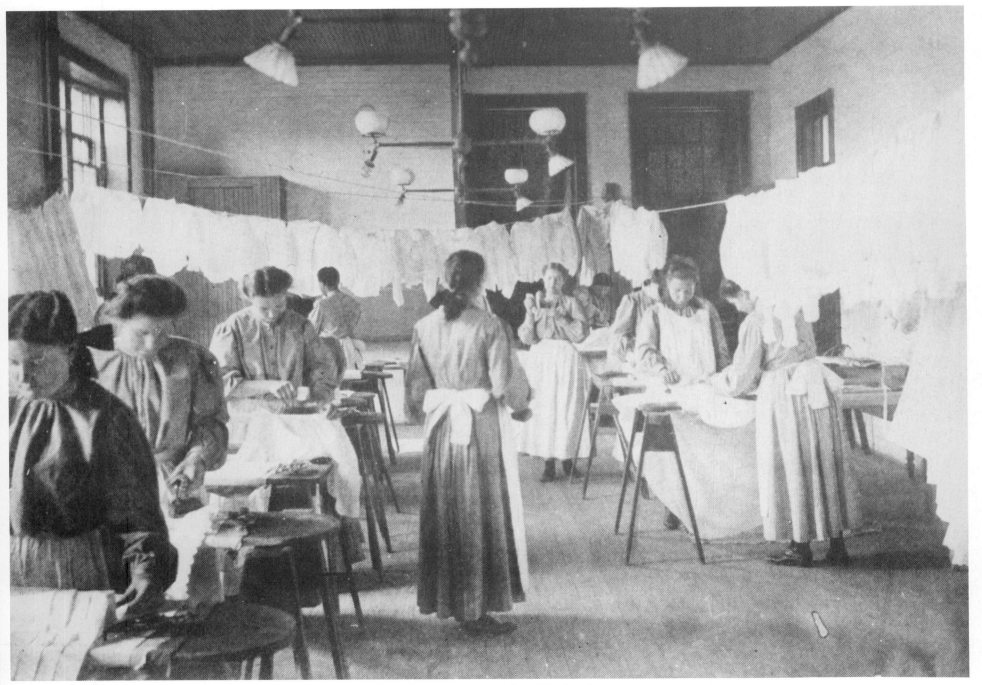

Ironing room, unidentified prison

Many other private and religious societies to help female offenders soon appeared in other cities. Among the most notable are the Women's Prison Association and the Hopper Home, both in New York. These societies established homes that were forerunners to modern halfway houses.

Christian, moral women provided female offenders with a place to live, religious and vocational instruction, and medical care. However, such societies and homes in which women supervised women were exceptions to the rule of male supervision of female inmates. In response, women reformers began to demand more female corrections professionals to push for Fry's program to be a permanent part of U.S. prisons and jails.

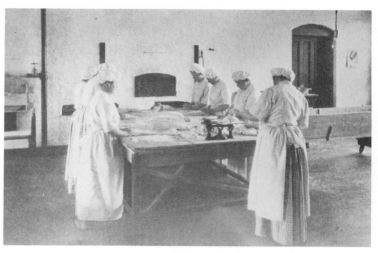

217   *Making bread*
Reformatory for Women, Sherborn, Massachusetts

218   *Kitchen of Women's Prison, Auburn, New York, c.1900*

219 *Women's Prison at Auburn, New York, opened May 29, 1893*

One of the few matrons for women between 1825 and 1873 was Eliza W. B. Farnham, a feminist, reformer, wife of a lawyer, and friend of members of the Brook Farm intellectual circle in Massachusetts. As head matron of the women's section of Sing Sing from 1844 to 1848, Farnham adopted Fry's program. She also tried to make the prison environment like a home in which staff and inmates behaved like a family. Believing that environmental conditions caused criminal behavior, Farnham changed the environment to facilitate behavioral changes. She ended the silent system; provided educational rather than religious instruction; and invited women from outside to speak to the inmates. Farnham's innovative programs and radical, secular approach met with criticism. After she was dismissed in 1848, her improvements were eliminated and conditions deteriorated.

220 *Ward in the Women's Prison at Auburn*

221 *Eliza W. B. Farnham*

169

Despite such setbacks, women's groups were able to convince male legislators to set up separate women's prisons and to hire full-time female superintendents and matrons. The first institution for women was the Indiana Reformatory Institution for Women and Girls, opened in 1873 with Sarah Smith as superintendent. Later, reformatories were opened in Framingham, Massachusetts (1877), Bedford Hills, New York (1901), and Clinton, New Jersey (1913).

Bedford Hills Reformatory for Women
New York, 1906

223   *Outdoor work*

222   *Disciplinary Building*

224   *Constructing a water tower*

225

*Nursery in Reformatory Prison for Women,
Sherborn, Massachusetts, 1904*

For years, pregnant inmates bore their children in prison. Usually, at about six months old, the infant was sent home to relatives or, if unwanted, put up for adoption.

Babies at the Connecticut State Farm and Prison for Women

A major assumption underlying the development of prisons for female offenders was that women are "naturally passive" and therefore not as dangerous as male offenders. This gave administrators of women's institutions more latitude in programming.

It is a little-known fact that many of the first female superintendents from 1884 to 1932, most of whom were well-educated and experienced in social work and reform, developed many correctional innovations. Such innovations include educational classes, libraries, art and music programs, work release, recreation, vocational programming, and classification based on behavioral criteria. Other "firsts" include Friendly Visitors, a community service volunteer group that still exists; a venereal disease clinic; and a center for studying the causes of female criminality.

228

229

230

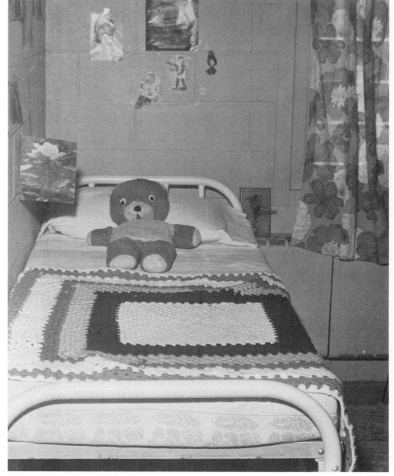

Early superintendents were faced with problems that still persist, including inadequate funding and difficulty in attracting high-caliber female professionals to work in institutions. In spite of such obstacles, early female administrators pioneered many important aspects of contemporary corrections.

**INDUSTRIAL
SCHOOL FOR GIRLS
BON AIR, VIRGINIA, 1939**

231

Furnishings of inmate's room:

1 Bed	$ 2.00
1 Mattress	3.70
2 Blankets at 2.00 ea.	4.00
3 Sheets at .25 ea.	.75
2 Pillow cases at .15 ea.	.30
2 Bath towels at .10 ea.	.20
2 Hand towels at .07 ea.	.14
1 Bedspread	.18
1 Laundry bag	.04
2 Wash cloths at .013 ea.	.03
1 Mirror	.75
1 Table lamp	.35
1 Pair curtains	.20
6 Hangers at .01 ea.	.06
1 Cup	.39
1 Comb	.07
1 Brush	.15
1 Toothbrush	.15
1 Bible	.35
1 Pillow	.56
2 Scarfs at .05 ea.	.10
1 Table	1.50
1 Wardrobe	2.25
1 Chair	2.00
	$20.22

232

***Training School for Boys
and Girls, Jamesburg, New Jersey***

Co-Correctional Facilities

The largest co-correctional facility in the United States is in Lexington, Kentucky. Bureau of Prisons research staff regularly monitor the Correctional Institutional Environmental Scale and have concluded that their studies "substantiate that co-correctional institutions do have a place in the prison system as a result of their unique capacity to provide a humane, nearly normal, safe environment.[1]

Research conducted by the Federal prison system[2] indicates certain aspects of incarceration appear to be consistent throughout co-correctional facilities—staff-inmate contact and interaction increases; inmates have a more definite role in their fate; inmates can talk to staff and still "do their own time"; and the environment is more normal than in a single-sex facility.

1. Bureau of Prisons, copy of Conference on Confinement of Female Offenders, March 28-30, 1979.

2. CEIS Research, Jerry Mabli, Ph.D., U.S. Bureau of Prisons.

174

233 **Federal Correctional Institution, Lexington, Kentucky**

234 *Playing backgammon, FCI, Lexington*

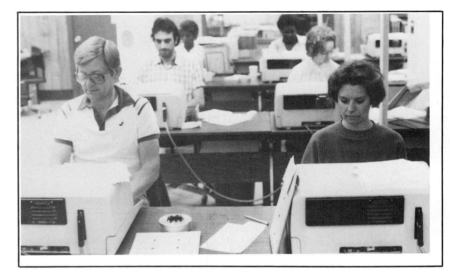

235 *Typing class, FCI, Lexington*

The female prisoner population in the United States has risen from 3,201 in 1925 to 17,649[1] in 1982, a rate exceeding the average population growth for the same period. The most alarming feature of this increase is the unusually steep rise since 1970, when the female prisoner count jumped from 5,430 to almost 15,000. In the 16-month period from March 1980 to June 1981, the U.S. male prison population was up six percent, while the female prison population increased by 10.6 percent.

This steady and consistent population increase, along with increased court interest and a desire by correctional officials to offer equal training and program opportunities to men and women in prison, has spurred new interest in female prisoners and facilities provided for them. From this interest the concept of co-correctional prisons has been developed in several states with varying degrees of success.

1. Bureau of Justice Statistics Bulletin "Prisoners in 1982."

The systems that continue to operate co-correctional facilities most successfully have established several basic patterns of operation, including:

1. The ratio of male to female inmates is as equal as possible, with neither sex allowed to exceed 65 percent of the total population.

2. Both male and female prisoners have less than two years remaining to serve on their sentences.

3. Offenders convicted of serious sex offenses or other extremely violent offenses are usually excluded from co-correctional facilities.

4. The institutional program provides for occasional furloughs or family visitation in the community.

5. A strict policy is maintained regarding transfer to a single-sex institution for improper behavior.

175

236

237

238

239

240

241

242

243

176 *Everyday Living, Industrial School for Girls, Lancaster, Massachusetts, 1926*

The Juvenile Offender

Cottage Group, State School for Boys,
South Portland, Maine, 1939

Although Americans have grown increasingly weary and intolerant of crime and criminals, no matter what their age, special facilities for juvenile offenders have been relatively slow in coming. The New York City House of Refuge, established in 1825, was the first noteworthy American response to the juvenile problem. Even then, courts had the option of sending juvenile offenders to adult prisons. Juvenile institutions were an attempt to protect offenders from the negative influences of adult offenders. Most of these institutions were actually schools established by private organizations and religious groups. In addition to working with juvenile delinquents, they focused on neglected and dependent children. The most popular system, cottage housing, began in Massachusetts (1854) and Ohio (1858).

It was not until **1899** that juvenile justice became a critical part of the country's criminal justice system, when the juvenile court system in Chicago was coordinated within a political jurisdiction.

Originally formulated to remove children from the punitive adult criminal justice system, the juvenile justice system has since expanded and now covers every jurisdiction in the country.

245

247

246

248

As a result, more standard patterns of confinement for juveniles have developed. Unfortunately, many jurisdictions do not have separate detention facilities for youths.

249

250

It is estimated that as many as 300,000 youngsters are held in adult jails and lockups each year. This is an acceptable practice under the statutory provisions of many states, as long as juveniles are segregated from adult offenders. The Juvenile Justice and Delinquency Prevention Act mandates separation of juveniles from adults in states receiving funds under the Act.

Like facilities for adult offenders, those for juvenile offenders are far from ideal. Like adult facilities, most are overcrowded, with an emphasis on custody; and most are isolated from communities by their structures and their security measures.

245-250   ***Scenes from Indiana Youth Center***

251

World War II

252 ***U.S. Penitentiary, Atlanta, Georgia, 1941***

253 *These model planes were used by pilot training schools to teach quick recognition of friendly and enemy craft*

The War Effort

The manpower and industrial demands of World War II supported a new correctional philosophy. Vocational training, primarily in supporting war production, rapidly spread throughout the system. This brought more qualified program staff, including psychologists, teachers, counselors, and recreational specialists, as well as growing numbers of volunteers.

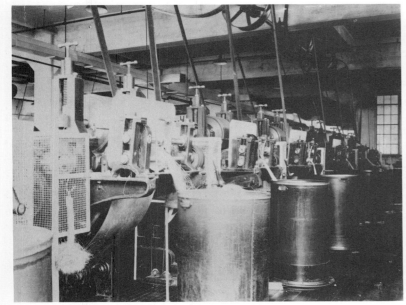

254 *Twine for defense, Wisconsin State Prison, Waupun*

255 *Making Army mattresses, U.S. Penitentiary, Atlanta, Georgia*

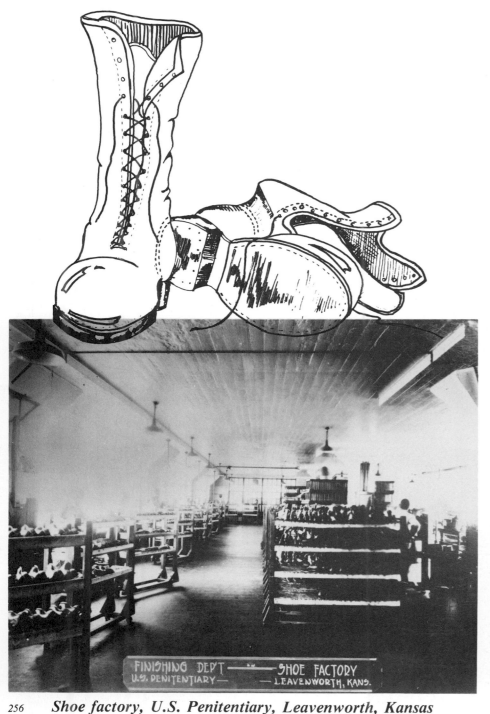

256   *Shoe factory, U.S. Penitentiary, Leavenworth, Kansas*

257   *Aircraft engine class, Federal Reformatory,*
Chillicothe, Ohio

Assembly line, Army assault boats, metal stamp plant, Michigan

The old adage that "prison made means poorly made" was disproved during the war years when vast quantities of prison made products met the rigid inspection requirements of all branches of the armed forces. Carloads of items poured from penal institutions to meet the urgent needs of governmental agencies during the emergency period.

259 **Tailor shop, Jackson State Prison, Michigan**

260 *Grinding steel billets at the State Reformatory, Rhode Island*

Items delivered under the wartime program by Prison Industries of Illinois included:

30,000	Maritime Commission Blankets
10,000	Treasury Department "Lend-Lease" Blankets
99,327	Yards of Treasury Department "Lend-Lease" Suiting
1,175	Coast Guard Office Chairs
40,482	Army Ordnance Department Shell Pallets
22,095	Army Ordnance Department Fuse Gauges for Shells
439,738	Navy Shirts—Blue Chambray
74,979	Treasury Department "Lend-Lease" Overalls
74,979	Treasury Department "Lend-Lease" Jackets
6,000	Army Unionalls
24,248	Army Shirts—"Bush"
49,534	Navy Shirts—"Sea-bee"
74,168	Treasury Department "Lend-Lease" Wool Trousers
104,190	Treasury Department "Lend-Lease" Work Shirts
78,024	Treasury Department "Lend-Lease" Denim Dungarees
6,008	Treasury Department "Lend-Lease" Denim Jackets
25,493	Army "Sun Tan" Jackets
26,451	Army "Sun Tan" Trousers
10,270	Army Khaki Trousers
819,862	Army Clothing, Canvas and Equipage Items repaired and returned to Army stocks
5,113,273	Army Clothing Canvas and Equipage Items segregated, classified and returned to Army stocks
5,214,100	Pounds of "Rough Dry" Army Laundry
1,395,423	Pounds of Army Laundry—Finished Work

These items represented nearly fourteen million production units valued at more than one and one-half million dollars; all products of prison labor and of prison shops under an industrial program that rapidly expanded as the government's needs became more urgent.[1]

[1]*Prison World,* May-June 1947
Article by Joseph E. Ragen,
Warden, Illinois State Penitentiary.

261 San Quentin inmates made model aircraft for use in identification classes; a part of military training. Aircraft range from the British Spitfire to Boeing B-17 heavy bombers.

262 *Prisoners engaged in textile production, Attica State Prison, New York*

263 **Rhode Island Reformatory inmates donate blood to American Red Cross**

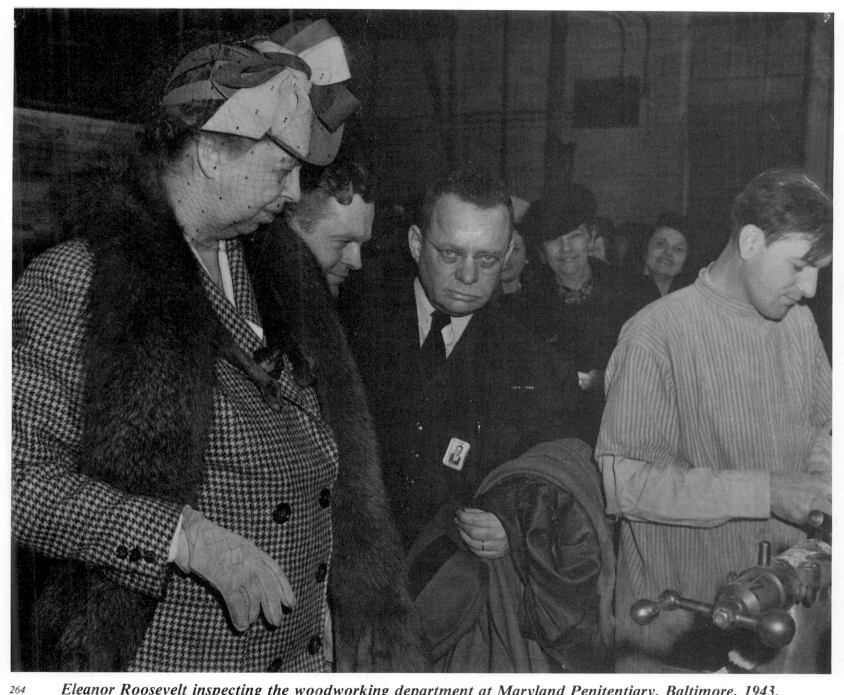

264 ***Eleanor Roosevelt inspecting the woodworking department at Maryland Penitentiary, Baltimore, 1943,
where furniture and bunks were made for the Armed Forces.***

265 ***San Quentin auditorium was used to assemble war ration books for civilian distribution, 1943***

189

In short, the prison was never to be the same isolated realm of the authoritarian warden and convict code. By 1950 the corrections field had expanded into an acceptable domain of study and social service. An entirely new group of professional personnel categories were introduced. Additionally, prison conditions became newsworthy. Attendees of the American Prison Association's Congresses were debating the potential of new programs and alternatives to incarceration. The Post-World War II period marked the end of massive prison war industry and training programs, but the needs of inmate programs in these and related areas were finally firmly established.

Parole Board meeting, Sing Sing, New York

The Box Score on the American Incarceration Rate continues...

267 *Main mess hall, Attica State Prison, New York*

Year	Number of Prisoners	U.S. Population	Prisoners per 100,000 Population
1950	166,000	151 million	110
1940	174,000	132 million	132
1930	148,000	123 million	121
1925	93,000	106 million	88
1918	75,000	92 million	82
1900	57,000	76 million	75
1890	45,000	63 million	71
1870	33,000	40 million	83
1860	19,000	31 million	60
1850	7,000	23 million	30
1840	4,000	17 million	24

Death row recreation, Texas

American Prisons, 1950-1970

VII

The offender was perceived as a person with social, intellectual, or emotional deficiencies who should be diagnosed carefully and his deficiencies clinically defined. Programs should be designed to correct these deficiencies to the point that would permit him to assume a productive, law-abiding place in the community. To achieve these goals of correctional treatment, it would be necessary only to maintain the pressure on the inmate for his participation in the treatment programs, to continue to humanize institutional living, to upgrade the educational level of the line officer, and to expand the complement of professional treatment and training personnel.

Perspectives on Correctional Manpower and Training, *Joint Commission on Correctional Manpower and Training, 1970*

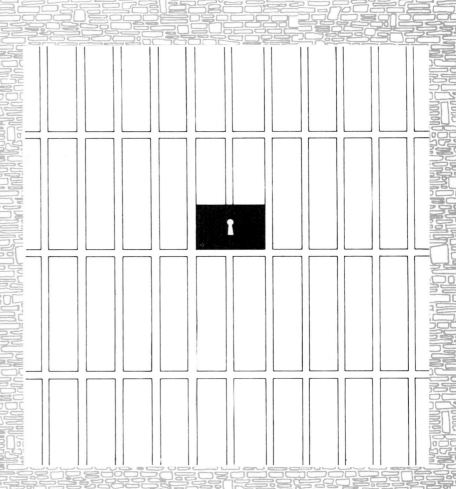

Classification

With **the evolution of correctional philosophy and in response to the humanitarian and Christian reform movements of the late 18th and early 19th centuries,** simple classifications of prisoners emerged. Correctional leaders were concerned about the ill effects of crowding prisoners together, particularly without regard for vast differences in age, type of offense, or mental state. Offenders also began to be segregated on the basis of the severity of their offense. Adequate medical care, work programs, and educational and vocational programs began to appear in prisons.

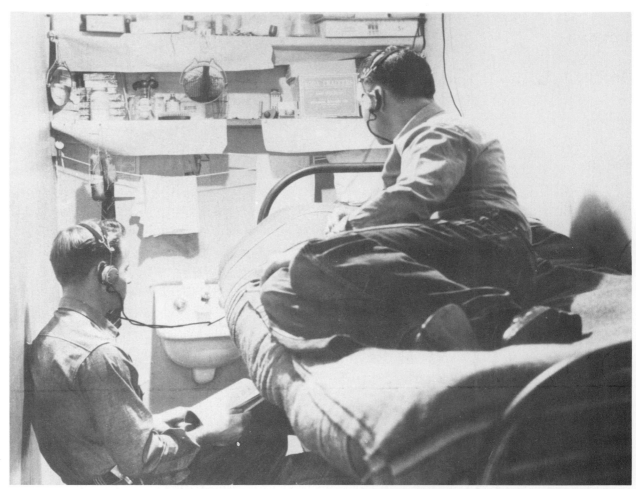

269   *Radio headsets in a San Quentin cell, California*

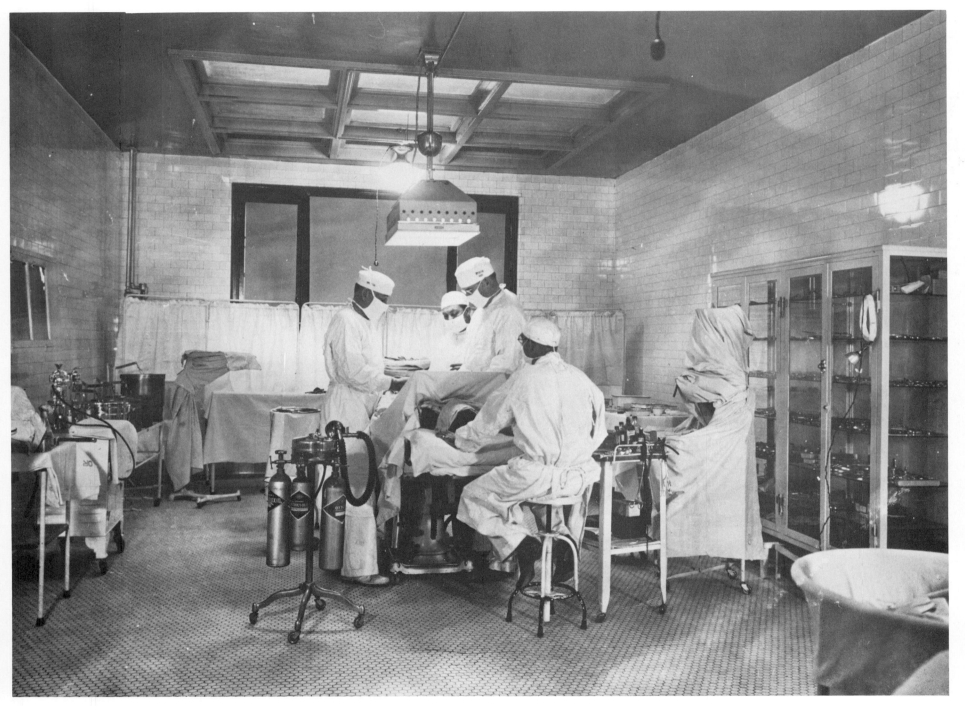

Operating room, Sing Sing Prison, New York, 1940s

Classification development moved into a second phase just before and after World War I, when correctional leaders started to apply the findings of the fast-developing social and behavioral sciences and began to train correctional workers in social work, psychology, and psychiatry. As a result, institutions set up clinics to screen and separate certain types of prisoners, such as the mentally retarded and the mentally ill.

271

272

Vocational training in linotype operations Federal Reformatory, El Reno, Oklahoma, top

Boxing match Utah State Prison Salt Lake City 1938, bottom

Classification meeting, New Jersey State Prison

By about 1930, the classification idea had expanded to include specialized screening and individualized treatment for all prisoners. Housing, treatment, and work assignments were made by institutional classification committees, based on the prisoners' medical, psychiatric, psychological, vocational, educational, sociological, religious, and disciplinary histories. Reclassification committees met at three- or six-month intervals to determine progress in the treatment plans and to estimate appropriate parole dates.

To make more efficient use of personnel and facilities, an increasing number of states began to develop centralized reception and diagnostic centers and specialized treatment institutions. Early classification planners hoped that classification information could be used primarily for rehabilitative purposes, but in practice it has been used more for management purposes. The current trend, however, is to emphasize helping offenders become responsible and to use classification as a means to that end. Correctional professionals use classification and treatment programs to modify offenders' attitudes and behavior patterns. There is considerable evidence that when a well thought-out system of classification is fully carried out, it is effective.

274   *Diagnostic Center in Menlo Park, New Jersey, 1950*

275

276

275-278 *STATE PRISON COLONY, Norfolk, Massachusetts*

Officially opened in 1931, this medium security, walled institution was planned for the more hopeful and adaptable men. Dormitory units instead of cell blocks provide a more spacious and less prison-like atmosphere. Considered the first "community prison" for males, selected inmates sentenced to other institutions are transferred to Norfolk to serve out their terms.

277

278

World War II was the maturation period of psychiatry and psychology, fields that developed into sciences considered capable of effectively dealing with emotional problems imposed by a world at war. Corrections embraced these disciplines and the word "treatment" was introduced in dealing with criminals. By differentiating prisoner populations into custodial or security groupings, some planned flexibility became possible.

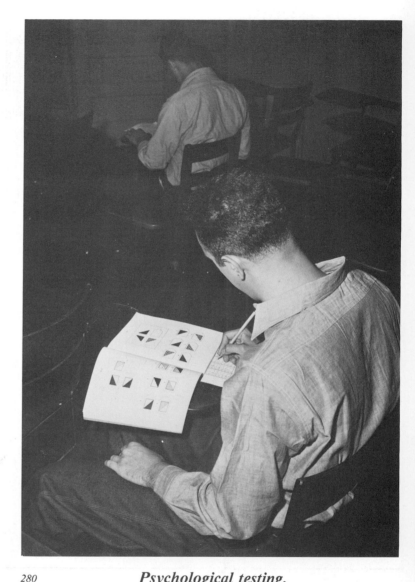

280 *Psychological testing, Elmira Reception Center, 1959*

Guidance Officer with inmate

Inmates eating cafeteria-style. In the past prisoners ate in enforced silence at long tables facing the same direction. Considering that inmates were often fed on a few pennies a day, sometimes going without fresh fruit for months, it is not surprising that the dining hall has been the setting for many prison disturbances. Today, inmates can converse at four-person tables, enjoying varied menus that take into consideration the culinary preferences of cultural groups and the dietary needs of inmates with special health problems.

281
"Chow line,"
Arizona State Penitentiary
Florence, 1971

282   **Federal Reformatory, Petersburg, Virginia, 1960**

202

283 *California Medical Facility,*
Vacaville, California, opened 1950

The "Telephone Pole" Plan

One of the first American facilities using the "telephone pole" plan was the Federal Penitentiary in Lewisburg, Pennsylvania, built in 1932 and designed by Alfred Hopkins. Facilities of this type flourished in the 1950s, as exemplified by Soledad, Tracy, and Vacaville in California; New Mexico Penitentiary at Santa Fe; the Marion and Lebanon Correctional Institutions in Ohio; Oregon Correctional Institution, Salem; Eastham and Ferguson Units, Texas; Massachusetts Correctional Institution, South Walpole; Connecticut Correctional Institution at Osborn; and Ontario Reformatory at Millbrook. This design accommodated new treatment programs while maintaining a strong emphasis on security regimens of the past.

285 *Alfred Hopkins*
1870-1941

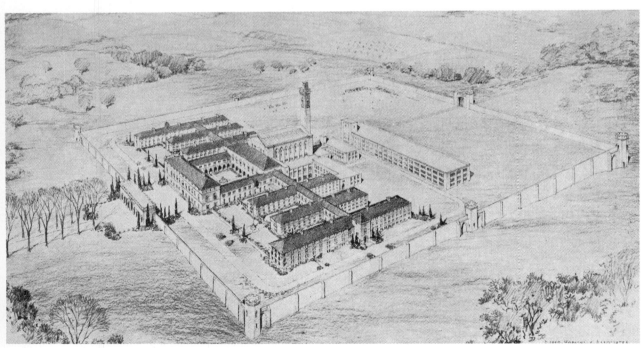

284 *Federal Penitentiary, Lewisburg, Pennsylvania*

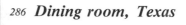

286 **Dining room, Texas**

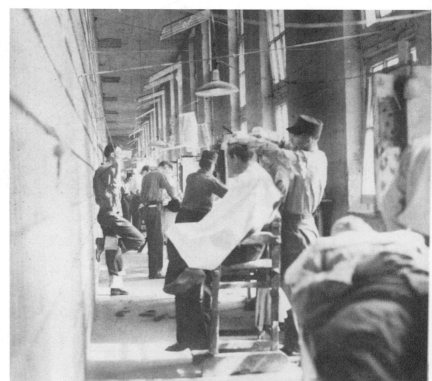

288 **First haircut in prison**

287 **Chapel**

The "telephone pole" design was centered around a long, central corridor. Cell blocks, dormitories, dining halls, the chapel, shops, schools, and administrative offices branched off the long corridor. The cell blocks, wings of three or four stories, had a new "openness" with floor-to-ceiling security windows.

289 **"D" Block**
Attica State Prison
New York 1954

290

Dining Area, Leesburg, New Jersey

Kulani Prison, Hawaii

Less Formal Facilities

During the late 1950s and early 1960s less formal correctional facilities began to emerge. New open institutions were tested as early as the 1930s, but only became a significant design concept with the construction of facilities such as the Michigan Training Unit at Ionia (1958), the Wisconsin Correctional Institution at Fox Lake (1962), and the Missouri Training Center for Men at Moberly (1963).

Riots and Disturbances

This period was plagued with riots. Between 1950 and 1966, over 100 riots and other major disturbances troubled American prisons. The eruption of major prison violence during this time heightened public awareness and paved the way for continued, extensive judicial involvement in the 1970s.

292 **Riot at State Prison of Southern Michigan**

293

294

The largest number of participants during a riot was at the State Prison of Southern Michigan at Jackson in April 1952, in which no hostages were lost and one inmate was accidentally killed.

The American Correctional Association investigated the riots and reported what appeared to be the main causes:

- Inadequate financial support and official and public indifference;

- Substandard personnel;

- Enforced idleness;

- Lack of professional leadership and professional programs;

- Excessive size and overcrowding of institutions;

- Political domination and motivation of management; and

- Unwise sentencing and parole practices.

.295 ***Inside exercise yard of the Segregation Unit at Huntsville, Texas***

This era of corrections is remembered most for its applications of the social and behavioral sciences, for the purpose of treating and rehabilitating offenders. Toward that end, new prison architectural designs were chosen to accommodate treatment programs, while maintaining security.

The Texas Prison Rodeo is held each Sunday in October. Proceeds are used entirely for the benefit of inmates.

296

211

297   *Wishing, Texas*

1970 to the 1980s

VIII

Many who advocate greater concern for prisoners oppose new prisons, arguing that judges will fill up the available cell space no matter how much it is expanded. Those fears are not unwarranted. However, the current situation suggests judges will fill up the space even when it doesn't exist.

Boston Globe
Editorial
May 1, 1981

Overcrowding: The Continuing Problem

Perhaps the foremost issue in corrections in the 1970s was whether to build more prisons. Overcrowding, a problem throughout the history of U.S. prisons, became an even greater cause of concern for correctional administrators. The nation's prison population had diminished during the 1960s, but the decline ended in 1968, when the national prisoner count was at 188,000.

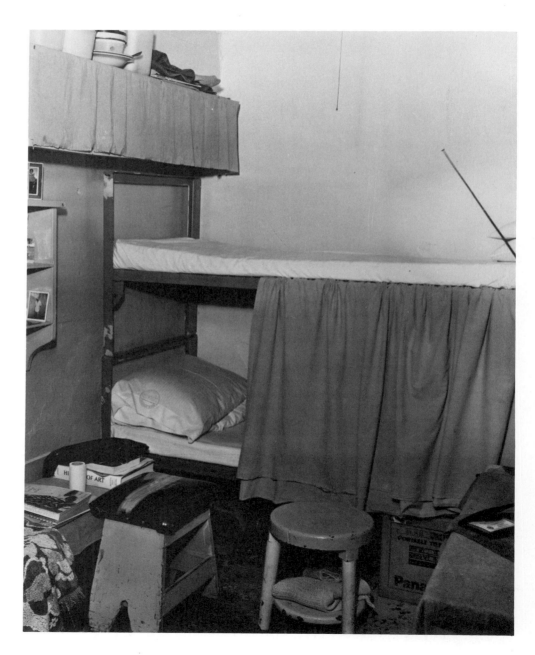

298 Double bunking,
Trenton State Prison, New Jersey

The Box Score continues...

Year	Number of Prisoners	U.S. Population	Prisoners per 100,000 Population
1970	196,000	203 million	97
1960	213,000	179 million	119
1950	166,000	151 million	110
1940	174,000	132 million	132
1930	148,000	123 million	121
1925	93,000	106 million	88
1918	75,000	92 million	82
1900	57,000	76 million	75
1890	45,000	63 million	71
1870	33,000	40 million	83
1860	19,000	31 million	60
1850	7,000	23 million	30
1840	4,000	17 million	24

By 1971, new commitments were up 35 percent over the 1968 figures. In 1972, sentence lengths began to increase somewhat, which in turn began swelling the number of prisoners at an accelerating annual rate. By December 1976, the prison population had surged 42 percent above the 1968 low and 36.4 percent higher than it had been in 1972.

One of the educational buildings, Sumter Correctional Institution, South Carolina, opened 1965

New prison construction could not keep up with this expanding population, leading to severe, widespread overcrowding that continues to this day, despite additional construction. And the numbers kept increasing. By the end of 1982, the nation's prison population reached an all-time high—412,000, compared to 196,000 prisoners in 1972.

300 *Vienna Correctional Center,
Illinois, opened 1965*

217

Landslide of Litigation

With the mounting overcrowding in prisons during the 1970s came a landslide of litigation. The prisoners rights movement that had begun in the mid-1960s gained dramatic momentum and brought judicial intervention into prisons.

The yard at the State Prison of Southern Michigan

In the 1970s the federal courts found nine state correctional systems to be unconstitutional in their operations. In January of 1982, 42 state systems (including the District of Columbia and the Virgin Islands) were under court order for overcrowding and conditions of confinement. Almost every aspect of correctional operations has been challenged and scrutinized: housing, health care, recreation, mail privileges, classification, and diet, just to name a few.

General population cellblock, Deuel Vocational Institution, California, 1976

Recent Significant Inmate Rights Cases

Until the mid-1960s, U.S. courts operated under a "hands off" policy that allowed correctional administrators to determine, basically without court interference, policies and procedures outlining inmate rights. With the abandonment of the "hands off" philosophy, case after case has been brought to court.

303   *Inside the Reception and Guidance Center at the State Prison of Southern Michigan, Jackson*

Below are three landmark cases; other important cases are currently under litigation.

Bell v Wolfish[1]

In this 1979 case, the plaintiffs—inmates of a federally operated, short-term custodial facility designed primarily to house pre-trial detainees—charged that the following practices were unconstitutional: (1) double-bunking; (2) enforcement of the "publisher-only" rule prohibiting inmates from receiving hardcover books that were not mailed directly from the publishers; (3) the prohibition against inmates' receipt of packages from outside the institution; (4) the practice of body cavity searches of inmates following contact visits; and (5) the requirement that pre-trial detainees remain outside their rooms during routine inspections by correctional officials.

The U.S. Supreme Court, however, found that each of the above conditions of pre-trial detention was constitutional because they were justified by the valid governmental objectives ensuring the detainees' presence at their trials and the effective management of the facility, including maintaining security, internal order, and discipline.

Rhodes v Chapman[2]

In an 8-to-1 ruling, the U.S. Supreme Court decided in this 1981 case that prison overcrowding is not unconstitutional. Dubbed the "one man, one cell" case, *Rhodes v Chapman* involved doubling up inmates in 63-square-foot cells in a relatively modern Ohio prison.

According to Justice Lewis F. Powell, Jr., who wrote the majority opinion, "The Constitution does not mandate comfortable prisons...(T)o the extent that prison conditions are restrictive and even harsh, they are part of the penalty that criminal offenders pay for their offenses against society."

The majority decision stated that it is up to the state legislatures and prison administrators (not the courts or correctional organizations) to determine the requirements of the Constitution. However, in a separate concurring opinion, Justice William J. Brennan, Jr., stated, "Today's decision should in no way be construed as a retreat from careful judiciary scrutiny of prison conditions."

Ruiz v Estelle[3]

Due to the pervasiveness of alleged substandard living conditions in prisons throughout the state of Texas, the Fifth Circuit Court of Appeals ordered complete reconstruction of the Texas prison system, including the appointment of a Special Master to supervise and monitor the defendants' implementation of the court-ordered decree.

The court held that the overcrowding in the Texas Department of Corrections was of such a magnitude as to amount to severe punishment. In reference to the holding in *Bell v Wolfish*, the Fifth Circuit Court stated: "Although the Supreme Court stated that there was no 'one man, one cell' principle lurking in the due process clause the Court specifically reserved judgement on cases presenting different facts."

1. *Bell v Wolfish*, 441U.S.520,60L.Ed2d 447,99S.CT1861(1979)

2. *Rhodes v Chapman*, 452U.S.337,69L.Ed.2d59, 101S.CT.2392(1981)

3. *Ruiz v Estelle*, 666F.2d854(1982)

A Series of Riots

Prisoners not only waged wars in the courts during the 1970s, but correctional institutions themselves were all too often battlegrounds. A long series of riots took place, repeating the episodes of the 1950s. The two worst ones taking place in Attica State Prison in the beginning of the decade, and in the New Mexico State Penitentiary at the end. Attica, New York, exploded in September 1971, ending with a death toll of 43, while the New Mexico State Penitentiary riot in February 1980 left 36 dead. These riots and tragedies resulted, in part, from a lack of resources and public interest.

304 Nevada State Prison riot, February 21, 1978, cell furnishings destroyed

305 *Vocational training, auto mechanics, Texas*

306 *Inmate student, Texas*

In the mid-1970s the punishment model regained popularity, which has continued into the 1980s. More offenders are being imprisoned for longer periods of time. Determinate sentencing is becoming more prevalent and mandatory sentences are increasingly being imposed for certain crimes.

Reintegrating inmates into society was a major concern throughout the 1970s. Realizing that most inmates are eventually released from prison, correctional personnel wanted to provide inmates with needed vocational and other skills to prevent them from returning to prison.

Prerelease, work release, educational release, work furlough, home furlough, and halfway houses were introduced to help inmates work their way back into the community. This effort was not easy for a number of reasons, notably, citizen resistance to such centers being in their backyards, coupled with the geographic isolation of most prisons.

223

307 **Inmate library, Texas**

Standards and Accreditation

To help prevent recurring confrontations both in the courtroom and correctional courtyards, correctional leaders moved to develop their own professional standards. Standards setting has been an ongoing, dedicated activity, starting with the American Correctional Association's *Manual of Correctional Standards,* first published in 1946. The standards setting efforts were given more impetus by the establishment of the Commission on Accreditation for Corrections (CAC) in 1974 by the American Correctional Association. Manuals of standards were published for all components of corrections, including, of course, prisons. Since then, numerous prisons have passed the stringent accreditation criteria as outlined in the *Standards for Adult Correctional Institutions* and other standards manuals. By the end of 1982, 238 correctional agencies/facilities were in the process of seeking accreditation, and 293 were accredited.

The standards address all aspects of the prison environment, including minimum space per inmate, health care services, diet, recreation, and education and training for inmates and staff. Standards and the accreditation process have been—and are—invaluable in improving correctional practices.

Nevertheless, corrections' central philosophy, the treatment or medical model of corrections, which had come to the fore in the 1960s, became an object of criticism in the 1970s. Rehabilitation efforts received a failing grade in 1974 by Robert Martinson after he summarized 231 research studies from 1945 to 1967. He found that "with few and isolated exceptions the rehabilitative efforts that have been reported so far have had no appreciable effect on recidivism." Two years later, however, Martinson argued that recidivism rates were less than one-third of the previous estimate.

308 **Accreditation meeting**

Visits

Are visits from family and friends a privilege or a right? This question has been debated continuously, but visitors have been allowed as early as the Walnut Street Jail, opened in 1790. Diligent, well-behaved inmates were allowed visits from close family members—but only once every three months, for 15 minutes, through two grills, and under the scrutiny of a keeper. Although visits are more frequent now (typically once a month), visiting procedures are not always radically different from earlier times. Limited visiting hours, restricted visiting rooms all make it difficult for inmates to maintain ties with the outside world. Also, most institutions are far away from large urban centers (where most inmates' families live), requiring long, expensive trips for visitors. All too frequently, family and friendship ties wither under these conditions. Correctional leaders believe family visits can help offenders maintain family ties and avoid recommitment to prison.

309

Visiting, Indiana Reformatory, Pendleton, 1938

Mississippi introduced family overnight visits in the United States in 1905 as a measure to help control large numbers of black prisoners. It was not until the early 1920s that the privilege was extended to all inmates in that state.

While provided more frequently in Latin America and European countries, private family visits have been recently introduced in California, New York, Connecticut, Washington, and Minnesota, as well as federal programs in Canada.

Supporters of private visiting claim it strengthens family relationships, reduces homosexuality among inmates, lessens tensions between officers and inmates, and reduces their isolation from the outside community.

Correctional administrators continue to explore ways of providing visits while maintaining security.

Visiting room, Deuel Vocational Institution, California, top

Inmate families are encouraged to visit and share picnic meals with inmates in the camp at the Federal Correctional Institution at Lompoc, California, bottom

Inadequate Facilities

Another critical concern was the inadequacy of existing prisons. Of the 113 maximum security state prisons in operation in 1971, six were built before the turn of the century. The latter held two-thirds of the maximum security inmates in 1971. Later in the 1970s and into the 1980s prison construction became big business. With more and more convicted criminals receiving longer prison sentences, the state correctional systems, as well as the federal system, needed to build new prisons and additions to existing facilities. The American Institute of Architects (AIA) reported that by early 1980, 726 federal, state, and local prisons and jails were being planned or constructed.

312

Education center, Federal Correctional Institution, Lompoc, California, top

Housing facilities located at Huron Valley Women's Facility, Michigan's only prison for women felons, bottom

228

313

314   *Montana State Prison*

315   *Women's Correctional Center, South Carolina*

16   *Maximum security units, Nevada State Prison, opened 1981*

317   *Model of the Minnesota Correctional Facility,*
Oak Park Heights

Newer ≠ Better

Correctional architectural **design is** getting away from old, fortress-type structures. More windows, fewer bars, rooms rather than cells, and closed circuit surveillance are in vogue. However, with surveillance by television and electronic gates rather than by correctional officers, some critics find the new architecture more dehumanizing than the old.

318 *Control Center Coffield Unit, Texas*

230

"End Prison Construction"

There have been those who, since the 1970s, have advocated ending prison construction. These advocates would reserve incarceration for violent offenders and divert most nonviolent criminals to community centers or restitution activities.

319 *Interior*
San Diego Federal Metropolitan Correctional Center
inmate recreation room built in 1974

In the meantime, judges keep sentencing criminal offenders to prison. A 1981 *Boston Globe* editorial stated:

"At some point prisoner rights advocates have to ponder whether their cause wouldn't be better served by some expansion in capacity. Only when the correction department has some flexibility, only when it is not absorbed in issues of control and prisoner movement can rehabilitation efforts have any reasonable chance for success."

The debate on whether to build or not to build has been going on since the Quakers designed the first prison in the United States.

A quiet moment

In 1977 volunteers on a rock-crushing crew from the maximum security unit at the Nevada State Prison in Carson City dug stones from a quarry within the prison grounds. After shaping the rocks, they used them to build a recreation area for inmates and visitors. Performing one of the most hated prison duties, these "rock pile" volunteers earned $10 a month.

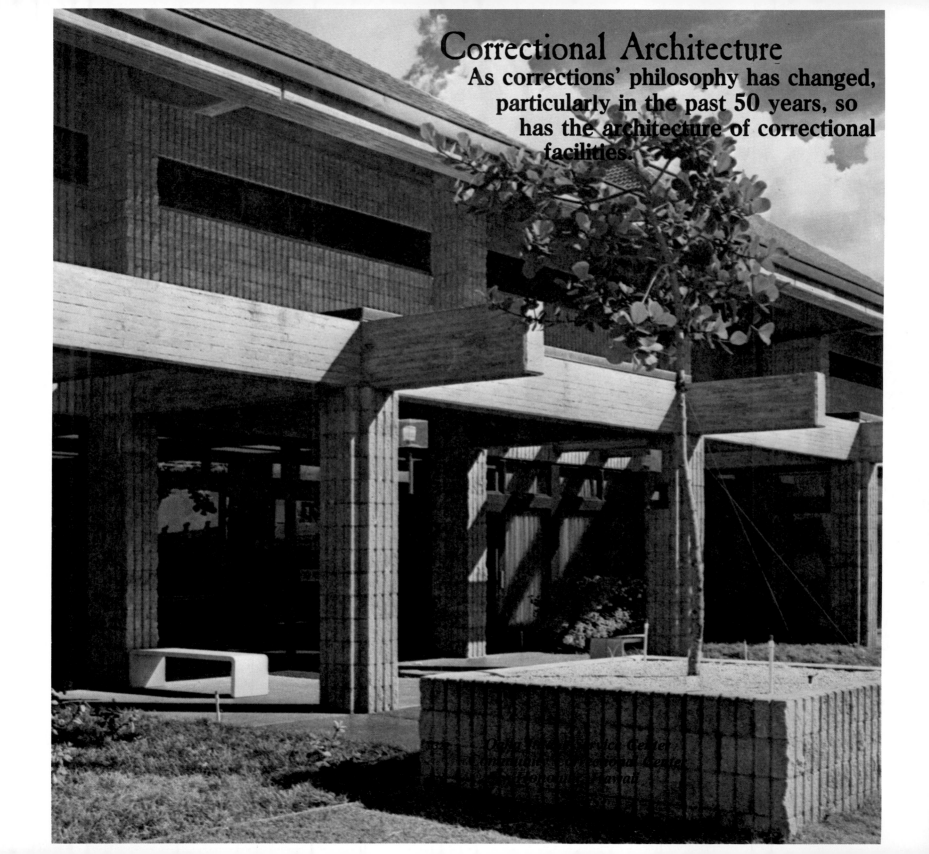

Correctional Architecture

As corrections' philosophy has changed, particularly in the past 50 years, so has the architecture of correctional facilities.

Oahu Community Correctional Center
Community Correctional Center
Honolulu, Hawaii

However, several dozen huge Gothic-style structures, built before 1900 with only economy, security, and isolation in mind, still stand, restricting the types of programs that can be offered. In contrast, the architecture of many contemporary facilities promotes flexibility in security and programming.

323

Federal Correctional Institution, Miami, Florida

324

Self-contained units are designed for small, compatible groups of residents, with each group having its own separate work, program, and outdoor recreation facilities. While these new facilities are far from "home, sweet home," they are certainly more humane for both staff and inmates.

235

325 *Modular facilities at the House of Corrections, Philadelphia, Pennsylvania*

326   *Medium Security Annex, Jessup, Maryland*

327 **North Carolina Central Prison**

Epilogue: A Look to the Future

By a coordinated criminal justice system, we can seek ordered liberty for all.
Anthony P. Travisono

328   *Inmate art*
Eagle by Lee Evans

The Torch of Resolution

Corrections today stands at the threshold of yet another era. Correctional practitioners of every generation have faced their challenges with hope and optimism, only to despairingly pass the torch of resolution to successors equally committed to resolving the correctional dilemma. Perhaps what is so strikingly different about modern corrections lies, to some degree, in the emerging attitude that corrections is the responsibility of all citizens, that prisons and jails belong to society.

The new philosophy calls for the involvement of "outsiders" if correctional efforts are to be effective. Corrections today reflects the thought and practice of numerous disciplines, each seeking to solve, once and for all, the recurring problems of punishment, deterrence, rehabilitation, and reintegration. None has resolved these problems, and change from one focus to another has been more a product of humanitarian impulse than of rational or scientific intent.

29 *Piedmont Correctional Facility,*
North Carolina

330

Piedmont Correctional Facility Control Room

Modern corrections, overlapping so many disciplines, including law, sociology, social work, psychology, education, recreation, and religion, has attracted the interest of increasing numbers of talented and dedicated professionals. Such interest is certainly needed. If current trends in arrest and conviction rates continue, corrections will be asked to cope with substantial increases in offender populations during the remainder of the 1980s—on top of current crisis levels of overcrowding in prisons and jails. Corrections will be hard-pressed in the decade ahead to confine these increased populations in a constitutional, humane, and acceptable manner.

The Incarceration Rate
Continues to Climb...

Year	Number of Prisoners	U.S. Population	Prisoners per 100,000 Population
1982	412,000	233 million	177
1980	321,000	227 million	142
1970	196,000	203 million	97
1960	213,000	179 million	119
1950	166,000	151 million	110
1940	174,000	132 million	132
1930	148,000	123 million	121
1925	93,000	106 million	88
1918	75,000	92 million	82
1900	57,000	76 million	75
1890	45,000	63 million	71
1870	33,000	40 million	83
1860	19,000	31 million	60
1850	7,000	23 million	30
1840	4,000	17 million	24

331

Richland County Judicial Center, South Carolina

332 *Whiteside County Law Enforcement Center, Illinois*

We must focus more attention on the conditions of incarcerated persons... To put people behind walls and bars and do little or nothing to change them is to win a battle but lose a war... It is wrong. It is expensive. It is stupid.

Chief Justice Warren Burger
February 1981

Correctional practice must deal simultaneously with the pressures of increased use of alternatives to incarceration, as well as traditional practices of institutional confinement, and it must do so with the paramount duty of protecting the public.

333   *Trenton State Prison*

WHAT OF THE FUTURE?

There are, of course, few certainties. The growing burden of corrections' social and economic costs will be massive, whether measured in dollars or human terms.

Corrections' future task must include increasing the public's involvement and acceptance. This entails building or rebuilding solid ties between offenders and the community, reintegrating offenders into community life, restoring family ties, obtaining employment and

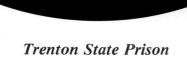

334 *Trenton State Prison*

education, and securing (in the larger sense) a place for offenders in the routine functioning of society. This will require efforts directed not only toward helping offenders change, which has been the almost exclusive focus of rehabilitation, but also mobilizing and changing the community and its resources. These efforts must be undertaken without giving up the important control and deterrent role of corrections, particularly as applied to dangerous, violent offenders.

335 *Interior, Trenton State Prison*

The Ultimate Goal

The ultimate goal of corrections is to do its share to increase community safety by reducing crime. Helping offenders accept personal responsibility to prevent their return to crime is, in general, the most promising way to achieve this end.

Protecting public safety does not necessitate incarcerating all offenders. Appropriate institutions and skilled, competent staff are scarce and should be used to provide confinement only for the most predatory and persistent offenders in a free and orderly society.

North Carolina Central Prison, Raleigh

337　*Module Control Room, Special Offender Center, Maximum Security Facility, Monroe, Washington*

Metropolitan Correctional Center, Chicago

Punishment

How should a society that espouses democratic ideals punish its criminal offenders? These and other questions remain unsolved and lack public consideration. Thorough rethinking of the nation's criminal justice policies and the role of prisons is needed as never before. A more comprehensive consideration not only addressing the legitimate aims of society and the authority of the law, but also recognizing and protecting the rights of the offender and the victim, must be forthcoming.

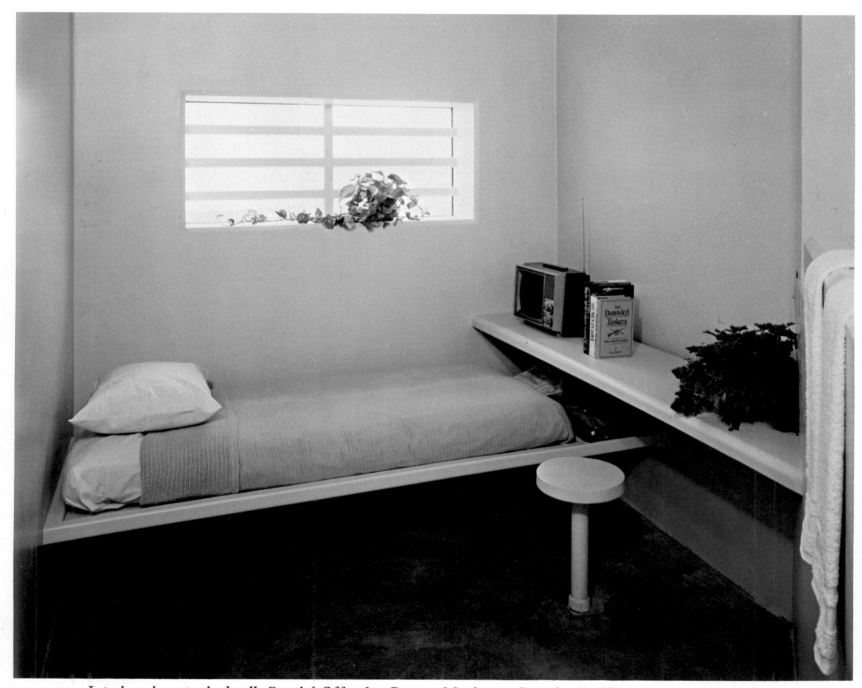

339 Interior view, typical cell, Special Offender Center, Maximum Security Facility, Monroe, Washington

Prisons will remain because society will continue to find crimes such as murder, rape, aggravated robbery, and other violent crimes abhorrent and will respond by removing such offenders from society. Justice in a democracy demands fair treatment of all citizens, neither ignoring victims nor degrading prisoners. As Franklin D. Roosevelt stated, "A nation does not have to be cruel to be tough."

340 Federal Correctional Institution, Butner, North Carolina

Clearly, there is a need for greater understanding and new and better responses. We must build a safe, humane, just, and effective system appropriate not only for the staff and offenders, but for our total society.

341 **Hiland Mountains Correctional Center, Eagle River, Alaska, 1982**

342   *Hiland Mountains Correctional Center, Dining area*

The Decades Ahead...

With dedication and determination, corrections may achieve in the decades ahead:

- A basic philosophy of corrections that is practical and rational;

- The phasing out of large maximum security prisons in favor of smaller, more manageable institutions staffed by well-trained, well-educated correctional professionals;

- Diversion of large numbers of offenders from traditional incarceration to programs for mental health, mental retardation, and drug addiction treatment;

- Greater emphasis on community-based programs for offenders who present minimal risk to the community;

- Expansion of offender restitution programs to compensate crime victims;

- Classification and risk assessment techniques that more adequately protect society, inmates, and correctional staff;

- Prison industrial work programs intelligently operated by the state or the private sector;

- Specialized correctional facilities for the care and control of long-term offenders;

- Selected offenders living with their families in a controlled environment as similar to a normal community as possible;

- An increasing role for society in the operation of correctional programs at all levels of government; and

- The provision of better information management systems to aid decision-makers.

343 Exterior view of housing modules
Medium Security
Deer Lodge, Montana, 1977

344　**North Carolina Central Prison, Raleigh**

345 *Medium Security Institution, Brunswick County, Virginia*

346 *Integration of the Old and the New, Trenton State Prison, Rehabilitation*

A New Generation

Finally, in the years to come, it is hoped that, spurred on by greater understanding, citizens will direct a new generation of correctional workers to create more positive chapters in corrections' history. For the harm done through their wrongdoings, offenders are responsible. But, for using inappropriate methods for treating offenders, when better methods are known, we are all guilty.

PHOTO CREDITS*

The American Correctional Association has collected photos throughout its 113-year history for various publications and research projects. However, records have not been diligently kept through several office moves. We feel most fortunate to *have* an archival collection of photos rich in the history of the American prison, but we have not always been sure of the source for some of these photos.

The Association has made every effort to properly credit the photos in this pictorial history of the American prison. If we have inadvertently overlooked any contributors to this collection, we humbly apologize.

We wish to acknowledge the courtesy of the following correctional departments, historical societies, and the Library of Congress as well as those anonymous contributors from the past.

ACA = Archives of the American Correctional Association
LC = Library of Congress
PPS = Pennsylvania Prison Society
FBP = Federal Bureau of Prisons
DOC = Department of Corrections

*All references are to photo numbers.

1 ACA: Photo by Shetland; **2,3** Reproduced from *Forging His Chains*, George Bidwell, 1889; **4** LC: Wood engraving in Harper's Weekly, Dec. 12, 1886. Sketched by Earl Shinn; **5** FBP.

Chapter I

6 FBP; **7** LC: Etching by Goya; **8,9** FBP: Reproduced from *Criminal Prisons of London,* Henry Mahew and John Binny, 1862; **10** FBP; **11** Reproduced from *Forging His Chains,* George Bidwell, 1889; **12** FBP; **13** Reproduced from *Forging His Chains,* George Bidwell, 1889; **14** LC; **15** ACA; **16** LC: Wood engraving by P. Meeder after A.R.W. in *The United States of America, A Pictorial History,* v.2, 1906; **17** ACA; **18** PPS: Reproduced from *New Horizons in Criminology,* Barnes & Teeters; **19** FBP: Reproduced from *Criminal Prisons of London,* Henry Mahew and John Binny, 1862; **20,21** ACA; **22-24** FBP: Reproduced from *Criminal Prisons of London;* **25** Reproduced from *Forging His Chains,* George Bidwell, 1889; **26** ACA.

Chapter II

27-29 Drawings by Marty Pociask; **30** ACA; **31** FBP; **32** LC: Wood engraving in Harper's Weekly, Dec. 5, 1868 after sketch by W.S. Sheppard; **33,34** Reproduced from *History of Newgate of Connecticut,* Richard H. Phelps, 1886; **35** FBP; **36-40** PPS; **41** FBP; **42** Reproduced from *American Bastile, John A. Marshall, 1878;* **43** FBP; **44** FBP, Benjamin Henry Latrobe, Architect; **45** NY State Commission of Correction; **46** MA DOC; **47** MD DOC; **48** NY DOC; **49** Reproduced from *Memorials of Prison Life,* Rev. James B. Finley, 1854.

Chapter III

50 FBP; **51-53** ACA; **54** Reproduced from *Warden Cassidy on Prisons and Convicts,* Michael J. Cassidy, 1897; **55** LC: "Implements of Torture, and Their Dangerous Effects," Illustrated by James Akin, 1833; **56** Reproduced from *Warden Cassidy on Prisons and Convicts,* Michael J. Cassidy, 1897; **57,58** ACA; **59-61** Reproduced from *Warden Cassidy on Prisons and Convicts,* Michael J. Cassidy, 1897; **62,63** Reproduced from *Memorials of Prison Life,* Rev. James B. Finley, 1854; **64** LC: Wood engraving in *The Illustrated London News,* February 16, 1876; **65** Reproduced from *The Trail of the Dead Years,* Earl Ellicott Dudding, 1932; **66** Correctional Service of Canada; **67** NY DOC; **68** LC: Engraving in *Historical Collections of the State of New York:* John W. Barber, 1840; **69,70** NY DOC; **71** IL DOC; **72** ACA; **73** NY DOC; **74** ACA; **75** IN DOC; **76** LC: Engraving in *Historical Collections of the State of New York,* John W. Barber, 1840; **77** FBP; **78,79** NY DOC; **80,81** IL DOC; **82** LC: Photo by A.J. Riddle, 1865; **83** ACA; **84** Reproduced from *United States Bonds,* Isaac W.K. Handy, 1874; **85** IL DOC.

Chapter IV

86 NY DOC; 87 OR DOC; 88 LC: Photo by Smith & Miller, 1896; 89 Cincinnati Historical Society; 90 ACA; 91 NY DOC; original photo in the collection of Warden Langhart, warden at Auburn in 1883; 92,93 ACA; 94 FBP; 95 ACA; 96,97 OH DOC; 98-103 NY DOC; 104-107 ACA; 108 NY DOC; 109 PA DOC; 110 ACA; 111 LC; 112 ACA; 113,114 LC; 115 LA DOC; 116 NC DOC.

Chapter V

117 LA DOC; 118 IL DOC; 119 KS DOC; 120-122 NY DOC; 123 LA DOC; 124 ACA; 125 IL DOC; 126-128 ACA; 129 IL DOC; 130,131 ACA; 132 NJ DOC; 133 ACA; 134 VT DOC; 135 ACA; 136-138 CA DOC; 139-144 ACA; 145 IL DOC; 146-151 ACA; 152 IL DOC; 153 LA DOC; 154-156 ACA; 157 OH DOC; 158 OR DOC; 159 OH DOC; 160 ACA; 161 IL DOC; 162 ACA; 163,164 IL DOC; 165 ACA; 166 IL DOC; 167 ACA; 168 NC DOC; 169 ACA; 170 FL DOC; 171 NY DOC; 172 WA DOC; 173 MA DOC; 174,175 NY DOC; 176 ACA; 177 NY DOC; 178,179 IL DOC; 180 NY DOC; 181 Photo by Ed Clark, LIFE Magazine© 1943, Time, Inc.; 182 NY DOC; 183 Minnesota Historical Society: Photo by H.R. Farr, Minneapolis; 184 OH DOC; 185 OR DOC; 186 CA DOC; 187 OR DOC; 188 Photo by Chris Troyano, *Hunstville Item;* 189 IN DOC.

Chapter VI

190 ACA; 191 FL DOC; 192 CA DOC; 193 ACA; 194 TX DOC; 195 ACA; 196 WA DOC; 197,198 NY DOC; 199 ACA; 200 IN DOC; 201-204 FBP; 205 IL DOC; 206 CA DOC; 207 IN DOC; 208 IL DOC; 209-211 NY DOC; 212 OH DOC; 213 Reproduced from *The New York Tombs Inside and Out,* John Josiah Munro, 1909; 214 IL DOC; 215,216 ACA; 217 MA DOC; 218-220 NY DOC; 221 New York Historical Society: Rephoto of a carte-de-visite photograph, c.1864; 222-224 NY DOC; 225 MA DOC; 226,227 CT DOC; 228-232 VA DOC; 233-235 FBP; 236-243 MA DOC; 244 ME DOC; 245-250 IN DOC; 251 ACA; 252 FBP; 253 ACA; 254 WI DOC; 255-257 FBP; 258,259 MI DOC; 260 RI DOC; 261 CA DOC; 262 NY DOC; 263 RI DOC; 264 MD DOC; 265 CA DOC; 266,267 NY DOC; 268 TX DOC.

Chapter VII

269 CA DOC; 270 NY DOC; 271 FBP; 272 UT DOC; 273,274 NJ DOC; 275-278 MA DOC; 279,280 NY State Health Department; photos by M. Dixson; 281 AZ DOC; 282 FBP; 283 CA DOC; 284,285 FBP; 286 TX DOC; 287,288 ACA; 289 NY DOC; 290 NJ DOC, Photo by David Hirsch, New York; 291 HI DOC, photo by R. Wenkam; 292-294 MI DOC; 295-297 TX DOC.

Chapter VIII

298 NJ DOC; 299 SC DOC; 300 IL DOC; 301 MI DOC; 302 CA DOC; 303 MI DOC; 304 Photo by Washoe County Sheriff's Dept., Reno, NV; 305-307 TX DOC; 308 ACA; 309 IN DOC; 310 CA DOC; 311,312 FBP; 313 MI DOC; 314 MT DOC; 315 SC DOC; 316 NV DOC; 317 MN DOC; 318 TX DOC; 319 FBP; 320 ACA; 321 ACA: Photo by Jay Aldrich of the *Gardnerville Record-Courier;* 322 Associated Architects and Engineers of Hawaii; 323,324 FBP; 325 Design Space International (DSI) Company; 326 MD DOC; 327 Hellmuth, Obata & Kassabaum, Inc., Architects.

Epilogue

328 Reproduced from a sketch by Lee Evans; 329,330 Henningson, Durham & Richardson, Architects; 331 GMK Inc., Architects; Photo by Gordon Schenck; 332 The Durrant Group, Inc.; 333-335 The Gruzen Partnership/The Grad Partnership, a joint venture—Michael Savoia, AIA partner-in-charge; Burton W. Berger, AIA, project director; 336 Hellmuth, Obata & Kassabaum, Inc., Architects; 337 Walker McGough Foltz Lyerla, P.S., Architects; 338 FBP; 339 Walker McGough Foltz Lyerla, P.S., Architects; 340 FBP; 341,342 Hellmuth, Obata & Kassabaum, Inc., Architects; 343 Walker McGough Foltz Lyerla, P.S., Architects; 344 Hellmuth, Obata & Kassabaum, Inc., Architects; 345 Henningson, Durham & Richardson, Architects; Photo by David Wilson; 346 The Gruzen Partnership/The Grad Partnership, a joint venture—Michael Savoia, AIA partner-in-charge; Burton W. Berger, AIA, project director.